D1603111

ASIAN FLAVORS

ASIAN FLAVORS

Oriental Cooking for Americans

Kay Shimizu

Illustrations by
LOIS SHIMIZU DENNIS

AN EXPOSITION-BANNER BOOK

Exposition Press   New York

EXPOSITION PRESS INC.

50 Jericho Turnpike   Jericho, New York 11753

FIRST EDITION

Library of Congress Catalog Card Number: 70-164869

0-682-47305-7

I truly dedicate this book:

To my most understanding and patient husband, Esau, who always allows me the liberty to be an individual, and to pursue whatever challenges I desire. Without having had this freedom and his heartfelt cooperation, I never could have accomplished the monumental task of writing this book.

To my daughter, Lois, who did the sketches with much love.

To other members of my faithful family—Glenn, Douglas, Allen, *et al.*—who, with dauntless spirit, tasted, then picked at or devoured, depending upon the results, the same food experiments day after day until I finally achieved what I was seeking. This has been going on for years—and we are still at it!

To my countless relatives, friends, and students, whose faith in me encouraged, inspired, and urged me on. I cannot begin to name them all.

To you, my unknown public, through these pages I extend my hand in friendship and good will, and a wish for many happy hours of good cooking and enchanted eating.

CONTENTS

●••●

PREFACE   9

INTRODUCTION   11

Shopping and General Food Preparation Hints   15
Menu Planning   16
Tips on How to Cook Asian Style   17
How Many Will the Recipe Serve? Will the Food Freeze?   19
How to Prepare Ingredients   20
Unique Oriental Cooking Methods   22
Authentic Tools and Utensils   24
Manners: Traditional? Modern? What Is the Approach?   30
Entertaining Asian Style for Americans   32
How-to Section   35
Hors d'Oeuvres   49
Fanciful Appetizers   52
Soups   66
Garnishes   70
Vegetables, Salads, Noodles   75
Poultry Dishes   99
Beef Dishes   115
Pork Dishes   123
Egg Dishes   137
Classic Japanese Dishes   143
Seafood Dishes   156
Bean Cake, Rice, Pickler   172
Desserts   188
Helpful Hints   201
Finale   213

INDEX   215

PREFACE

Although American-born and educated, and thoroughly Western in my way of life, the Oriental foods of my Asian heritage have always intrigued and challenged me, and for more than twenty-five years, when few books on the exotic cooking you are about to experience were available, I have been persistently researching, studying, testing, and tasting until I have mastered the art of Oriental cookery.

I have made no attempt here to cover all there is to know about either Japanese or Chinese cuisine, for this would be an impossible task to accomplish in one volume of this size. We all like to prepare fare that will please our ego as well as our palate, and with this in mind, I have included in *Asian Flavors* the simplest recipes retaining the authentic flavors of the Far East. Many of my dishes may seem formidably exotic to the beginner or too impractical, while others may appear to be too plain. Don't be deceived. All may be easily prepared in your own kitchen and in fact, the plain looking ones often are the most appealing.

My recipes are not methodically grouped in particular sections. They are, rather, unconventionally and esthetically blended together, hence, you will find Chinese and Japanese dishes intermingled with an occasional "American cosmopolitan" idea. Combine them to create original specialties of your own and let your personality shine through. My directions are as explicit as though I were right in your kitchen directing you, so don't hesitate—be daring, be confident, believe in yourself—you can become the fabulous cook you have always wanted to be!

When I began to teach professionally in adult cooking classes I was amazed at the enthusiastic reception accorded. Today, I am still awed by the great interest and eagerness that prevails. To be able to meet so many thousands of individuals and to help them in the joys of Asian cooking, to touch their lives in such a beneficial, healthful way, to hear students say, "My husband thanks you for this course . . ."; "My whole family loves vegetables now . . ."; "I prepared an eleven-course Oriental dinner party and all went well . . ."; fills me with pride and warmth. It is my sincere desire to continue sharing my knowledge and offering to everyone the results of my experiences.

You will see as you "work" through this book it is not just cooking but a kind of *handbook*. The calligraphy—brush writing —is a most exquisite art form of Oriental expression. The circular crest design of ivy leaves is our Shimizu family's treasured symbolic mark dating back centuries ago in Japan. Enliven your life with my shared cultural offerings.

My heart is like fire—burning to spread the fun of Asian cooking to you. So join me as we venture on a most exciting pathway to Oriental cuisine—adapted especially for *you*.

KAY SHIMIZU

INTRODUCTION

As travel has become more extensive, and other countries have become more accessible to the average person, we have become interested in our foreign neighbors' way of life and eating habits. This book tells you a great deal about them, but cookbooks, like all books, are only the printed histories of man's accomplishments in a chosen field. Learning to be proficient yourself means continual practice. This is especially true of Oriental cuisine because it is so totally different from European or American cooking.

Many of the finer points of cooking can be learned only in a classroom or by observing an experienced cook, when details can be gone over, questions asked and answers given. If there are cooking classes offered in your area, by all means, enroll if it is at all possible. Meanwhile, there is much to learn from *Asian Flavors.*

The Orientals have a unique culture, centuries old in tradition and heritage—a heritage they respect and adhere to in every way, especially in the preparation and the eating of their food. When preparing a meal they proceed with ritualistic serenity and with almost rustic simplicity, using their ingenuity when needed.

Both Chinese and Japanese foods are some of the healthiest a person can enjoy, and among the tastiest when properly prepared. Asian food, on the whole, is diet-oriented, but there are few of us who can resist the tantalizing aroma and magnetic draw of deep fat-fried *tempura, won tons,* or the like. We can indulge in these rich dishes from time to time if we balance them with fat-free, low calorie fare. Confucius wisely preached way back in 500 B.C., that to eat two-thirds vegetables and one-third meat results in good health and long life. This is good advice for today as well.

A creative art, Asian cooking can be as eloquent as the artisan who produces a beautiful piece of ceramic—it will have as fascinating an appeal, but to more of your senses: tantalizing in taste;

clear, natural, bright to look at; irresistible, penetrating aromas; and wonderful nutrition so necessary for the nourishment of our precious bodies.

Cooking time is of the essence, especially in Chinese recipes, and in many Japanese dishes as well. Observe it, and you will have triumph after triumph. In Oriental cooking vegetables remain crisp and may seem underdone according to our American standards. So, even when cooking Oriental style, cook to suit your taste. If you like it sweeter or saltier than the recipe calls for, it is your prerogative to alter the proportions in accordance with your taste. Then too, your family may prefer certain vegetables to others. You may have dietary problems to cope with. Some people you are cooking for may not appreciate foreign foods. But you are the creator in your kitchen and you can overcome these handicaps. Do it!

Flavors are transformed with just a spoonful of this or a pinch of that. And what miracles can result from these sometimes strange-scented condiments! In addition, the utmost in love and affection must go into your cooking. Take a special interest in the simplest dish and it will become a truly outstanding miracle. The infinite variety to choose from in Chinese and Japanese foods will enhance your whole outlook on eating and will definitely alter your family's daily diet for the better. The dull monotony and apathy toward meals will disappear.

Not everyone has the ability to evaluate flavors. Outstanding flavors make an indelible mark on one's senses, but as you become more gifted I promise you that you will improve in this area. I hate to look back at what *I* thought was Asian cooking twenty-five years ago!

A word of warning! *Do not over-do the soy sauce.* It can be so overwhelming that true meat, fish, poultry and vegetable flavors will vanish. Use soy sauce sparingly, combined with ginger and other spices, and your food will take on a heavenly fragrance and flavor.

I am all for dining out and eating professionally prepared dishes from time to time. Go to a good Oriental restaurant periodically. Try different items on the menu. In this way you can learn to evaluate your own cooking. Beware though, of the restaurants who cater to Occidentals and serve what they think they want to eat. Go where the Orientals are for authenticity.

There is no substitute for practice and it was only through sheer determination and continual experimentation that I arrived at my goal. And I continue to learn—from many books, from practice, from friends—and keep adding to my repertoire daily. This applies not only in the cooking field, but in every area of living. Knowledge is power, and life is much more fun because of it. It is never too late to learn. Admit to yourself that you do not know it all and you will always improve. But do not ever apologize for your cooking! Tell everyone that you are the fantastic cook you will someday be. If your house is the cluttered up, lived-in kind, just lower the lights, use candles, and freshen the air when having company, and no one will notice anything but your delicious food.

Chinese food tastes different in different parts of the world. Each locale uses what is readily available, yet authenticity is more or less retained. With the availability to us, however, of so many of the original ingredients, including fresh Oriental vegetables and genuine condiments from the Orient, a certain consistency should be maintained no matter where the cooking is done or who does it.

Generally, Japanese foods are sweeter and sometimes saltier than Chinese foods. There is not quite the infinite variety that exists in Chinese cooking flavor-wise. In recent years, Western foods have invaded Japan and a slight change has occurred in the eating habits there. More meat and dairy products are being used. Some newer adaptions are poor imitations of our American foods. Use your own best judgment on this type of recipe. They are apt to be very "Japanesey."

I must remind you that just because you are all "gung ho" for Oriental foods do not serve them everyday. The sheer novelty and the mystery will disappear. We are fortunate that we have access to European, varied regional American style as well as Oriental foods—so be cosmopolitan and vary your daily menu as I do.

But be practical in your planning, and do the best you can under any circumstances. Embellishments can do wonders too.

Place a graceful bamboo branch on the side of your platter, a maple leaf along with the plate or even a cherry blossom by the raw ingredients. On top of the raw ingredients, it is most charming to place a fresh carnation or iris to be given to a lady guest to take home as a memento of the dinner. She will love it and treasure the thought. In these days of plastic and paper make-believe flowers, a whiff of fragrant perfume from fresh flowers is a welcome surprise. One of the popular country-style restaurants in San Francisco does this and I always love it there, especially for this innovation.

SHOPPING AND GENERAL FOOD PREPARATION HINTS

The basic Oriental cooking methods you will have to learn are to undercook, underchop, and undersoak the vegetables and the meat. No cooking of ingredients for hours (except for some regional type dishes which I do not cover in this book). The meat, fish, shellfish and poultry recipes here are most imaginatively prepared—with so lusciously tender, delicate and tasty results.

Before you try any recipe on company make a few trial runs, so that you will have perfected your cooking ability as well as adjusted flavors to your tastes. There is no substitute for practice. Have confidence and you will be able to cook Oriental style. This will soon lead to the pleasure of eating elegant foods. Enjoy yourself. And substitute intelligently—nothing is so rigid that you must be so exacting in Oriental cookery. This relieves the monotony of daily eating. Remember we eat on an average of ninety thousand meals in a lifetime.

Take advantage of what you find fresh at the markets. If asparagus is in season, use it in place of broccoli. Substitute only similar type vegetables. Do not use firm cooking varieties for soft, watery types, such as celery in place of tomatoes. You may get a disastrous and, definitely, a different flavor. Miracles and original creations do appear by substitution of many vegetables but one has to be inventive and with practice you will be making up your own combination before long.

I cannot stress enough the need to buy the best quality ingredients. It is only what you put into a dish that you will get out of it. The Orientals get the most out of every piece of meat, every variety of vegetable and so forth. Even with the abundance and variety available in America we should use our foods more wisely. It will save you money in the long run.

MENU PLANNING

When planning your daily menus, try to incorporate many Oriental foods along with your Western foods. You will be amazed at the compatibility of a Jello or green salad with certain Oriental flavors. We are a melting pot of many cultural exchanges, so learn to combine all sorts of dishes at your meals, such as a Chinese toss-fried dish, or a Japanese style vegetable with an American gelatin salad. Top it off with fresh fruit for dessert. Rice and tea, of course. Somehow, bread just does not go too well with many of the Oriental foods except for the broiled meats, fowl and some fish productions.

WHAT IS A GOOD ORIENTAL MEAL?

Naturally, using all Oriental dishes is fine, too. You could select many dishes that go nicely together. Keep a good balance in meats, fish, poultry and vegetables. Crispness, tenderness, smoothness and softness should all be distinct. Contrasts in color, texture and flavor are important, too. Sweet, sour, salty, bitter and fragrant are the basic flavors, especially of the Chinese. Try to keep your cooking less oily than many Oriental cookbooks suggest. I have found that food is satisfactory in flavor without using so much oil.

Apply these principles to all your cooking, be it Oriental, European or American, and you will enjoy cooking more.

Being hungry several hours after an Oriental meal indicates that little rice was consumed. Steamed rice is the bulk for your meal. It is like bread at our American table. The rice will "stick to your ribs." If you eat in moderation, it will not make you fat.

TIPS ON HOW TO COOK ASIAN STYLE

Speed, good organization and planning make for efficient Oriental cookery. The right tools help a lot too, but are not necessary to produce good meals. They certainly make cooking more enjoyable.

There is no deep mystery to Oriental cookery. Read your recipe over thoroughly so that you will know your ingredients and will have purchased everything necessary. Many of these ingredients are not common in every household, but by the time you have tried some of the recipes in this book, you will probably have most of the necessary spices and flavorings on hand. Learn your sequences and you will soon be inventing your own combinations!

Please remember that Oriental cooking is not cheap—you will discover that many things are most expensive, especially since many are imported merchandise, but a little goes a long way.

To begin, assemble all ingredients neatly in a 9 by 12 inch pan or large platter. Measure out and mix the gravy ingredients in a small bowl or clean can (so you can toss it out and save on dish washing). Then bring everything to the stove in one grouping. You will be able to cook much easier. You will find particularly in Chinese toss-fry cooking that you do not have time to start looking for this or that. Assembling all the ingredients first also assures that you will have the right sauce for the right dish. For Japanese cooking, in particular, place all the ingredients on a platter attractively—almost like a rhythmically composed picture as you cut—artistic appreciation of your raw ingredients is part of Japanese cuisine. Leave the cut pieces in the exact shape that nature gave it to us. Do not separate the onion rings, for instance, leave intact. For Chinese cooking, however, there is more stress made that all ingredients be consistently about the same size and shape for any one given dish. This is to allow the same cooking time for everything used for that entree. There is definitely, a uniform look to their dishes. If something is cubed then everything else is cubed and so on. There is not quite so much concern about the arrangement of the raw ingredients, since most of the time, it is toss-fried anyway. But it never hurts to apply some of this Japanese influence to the Chinese manner. You will find that there is much that I mix from the two Oriental cuisines, taking the best from each. In Chinese cookery, separate the vegetable pieces so that everything will be loose and free, such as onion slices—separate the half rings so that they will be individual strips of onion. I usually transfer the sliced items on the wide blade of my cleaver to the tray where I put all my ingredients, then with my fingers I loosely toss the vegetables to separate.

Japanese cuisine actually offers some leisurely preparation and cooking time since many of their foods are cooked ahead and consumed at room temperature. Chinese cooking, generally, is more last minute type, although there are exceptions in both countries.

With conviction and enthusiasm, the modern American will find Oriental cooking is not as difficult as it may seem. Get whatever you can prepare early out of the way, cover with plastic wrap and put in the refrigerator. Close to dinner hour, it is much less of a rush-rush feeling to know the main job of cutting and organization is finished. Get the rice cooked (often in the modern electric rice cooker) and the entree or entrees do not take too much cooking time. In fact, with some Oriental meals, you can get the guests to prepare the entree at the table.

I have often planned a many-course dinner and prepared it with ease. I may have three *woks* and a steamer going at once but with skill and experience one can do all these things without going out of your mind! You will become quite efficient as you perfect each dish, practicing until you know how to do it without referring to the directions. You can even begin to improvise a bit on the methods and the preparation of the ingredients, but start out learning the right way!

HOW MANY WILL THE RECIPE SERVE?
WILL THE FOOD FREEZE?

The majority of the recipes in this book will serve 3 or 4 persons with average appetites, if it is the only entree prepared along with rice and perhaps a salad. They will serve more persons, if a variety of dishes is made up and served family style in true Oriental manner. In Chinese cooking, especially, many entrees are prepared and everyone shares from the central serving dishes.

Some recipes suffer if increased beyond the proportions given. In special cases, I have marked the recipes if they cannot safely be doubled or tripled. This is very true with the use of certain seasonings. Too much of any special one, especially soy, can ruin the original intended flavorings and aroma and the grand dish you were going to prepare will be a disaster! It is safest not to increase the measurements until you are more familiar with Asian flavors and textures.

Freezing of certain foods is possible with some loss of flavor and texture. Often crispness is lost but the flavor will remain. There is no good substitute for freshly made Oriental foods, especially Chinese toss-fried entrees.

This book is meant for family-style cooking and not for you to use as a primer to start a restaurant. But if it does inspire such an enterprise, more power to you!

HOW TO PREPARE INGREDIENTS

These are the basic characteristics of ingredient preparation for both Japanese and Chinese cookery. The Japanese keep most of their ingredients intact and do not separate onion half slices, for instance. They maintain the shape that nature intended the vegetable to have, whereas the Chinese method is to separate the same onion half slices into a loose mound of half rings. Their

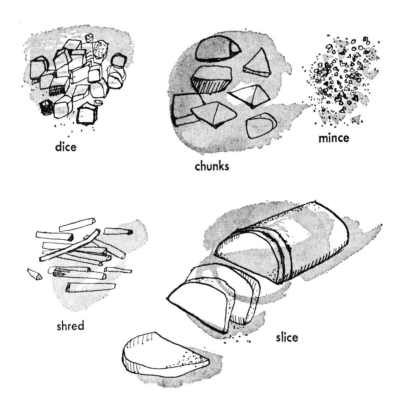

dice

chunks

mince

shred

slice

theory being that ingredients cook evenly when they are uniform as much as possible, in size and shape, in any one given recipe.

Grate—rub on grater—what else?

Mince—very, very fine. Chop with knife or two knives similar to the Chinese cleaver, until the mass looks like ground meat. Chopping helps the meat to retain juices. (Grinding smashes the meat and loses juices.)

Shred—fine, thin matchstick strips.

Chop—very small uniform pieces.

Dice—cut into ¼-inch cubes.

Slice—cut into slices ¼-inch or ⅛-inch by 2 inches, depending upon the recipe.

Diagonal cut—gives more of an Oriental look and exposes more surface for fast cooking—more aesthetic, too.

Oblique chunks or rolling cut—roll vegetable as you cut off thick pieces. Try it with a carrot and you will immediately get the idea.

UNIQUE ORIENTAL COOKING METHODS

STIR-TOSS FRYING

This is closest to sautéing in a heavy skillet. This is a cooking style entirely characteristic of Chinese cookery alone. The ingredients are vigorously tossed and cooked very briefly, only 2 to 5 minutes, over the highest heat. If your heat source is not very hot, you will have to adjust and take a little longer cooking time. A Chinese *wok* is excellent for this but certainly not essential. The best results are obtained when everything can be sizzling hot and cooked fast!

DEEP-FAT FRYING

The same as any other deep-fat method. Using a *wok* filled with vegetable oil heated to 350°F.-375°F. has advantages since there is little spatter and spillage. Do not fry too much at once since the oil temperature will be lowered. The secret is to maintain a controlled oil temperature. I prefer a bland, light vegetable oil for all frying. You can use any kind of heavy pot for this method.

BRAISING OR SIMMERING

A slow, stewing process. Often the objective is to tenderize and to harmonize the flavors thoroughly. The Japanese use this method for many dishes but shorten the time, cooking just enough to flavor the ingredients and to retain the crisp, crunchy texture— often only 3 to 5 minutes.

STEAMING

Cooking with a vigorously boiling pot of water furnishing the steam that circulates around the food being prepared. Oriental steamers have many layers of deep pans (often bamboo) placed one on top of another over a pot of briskly boiling water. I especially like the clean-looking Japanese shiny aluminum steamer pans since they are easy to clean and do not acquire the musty smells that bamboo ones eventually do. They come in sets that fit into the *wok*. You can improvise a steamer by using a turkey roaster or large pot. Place a tuna fish can with both ends removed inside the pan. Fill with water up to one-half inch below the can. Place your pyrex dish on top of the can when the water is boiling vigorously. Cover tightly. Another method is to use a colander inside of a pan.

PARBOIL

To scald or blanch in boiling water. Cooking can be stopped by passing through some cold water. The Japanese utilize this method very much in their cooking of vegetables. The clear, brilliant colors of the natural produce are retained this way, as well as much of the original vitamins.

HIBACHI COOKING

Cooking over charcoals in a special barbecue container. One could always use a makeshift container to achieve the same results. I have heard of persons using a wheelbarrow to build a charcoal fire, as well as a clean clay pot. Use your imagination!

AUTHENTIC TOOLS AND UTENSILS
(Do You Need Them or Not?)

Authentic tools and utensils are handy but certainly *not* essential for Asian cooking. You can produce Oriental food under almost any circumstances, perhaps not as exquisitely at times, but good food for good eating! I even prepare Oriental foods on camping trips—it surely beats heating the usual dull canned chili or stew! Why give up your gourmet tastes because you are on vacation (especially, if you still are not on vacation from the cooking chores)? The neighboring campers have even asked us: "What were you cooking? Smelled elegant!" We had dined on *teriyaki*. Freeze your flank steaks, chicken all cut up, partially prepared dishes, and so on. All can be cut ahead, frozen, and stored in plastic bags for days in your portable ice chests. Go on your trip with a *wok* and faithful cleaver. You can cook anywhere—on a stove or on an outdoor fire pit.

Some utensils I find essential, if speed in preparation is to be mastered. In these times speed is of utmost importance, as well as for the cook's convenience.

CLEAVER

A crude, rustic looking Chinese cleaver is primarily for slicing and chopping meat and vegetables Chinese-style. I use it, though, for Japanese, European, and American-style cooking. What a knife! Fantastic! You do not have to buy all kinds of knives— one for meat, one for vegetables, one for this or that. This is the only knife you will need to start with, and it is relatively inexpensive so far as good, efficient cutlery goes—only about three dollars. There are various weights, depending upon the thickness of the blades. Some are primarily for chopping, some are especially for slicing and others are for a combination of uses. You will discover that you can sharpen this knife very nicely on an old-fashioned hone. *Never* use an electric knife sharpener on it! Sometimes, the Hong Kong manufacturer has forgotten to sharpen the knife before shipping it, so you will have to do it before using. I usually sharpen only one side of the blade to lessen chances of cutting myself. (Housewives are notorious for accidents with super sharp tools.) This cleaver is far lighter than a French chef knife and I never tire of handling it. Always dry thoroughly after washing. Do not worry if it rusts, just scrub and the rust will wash away. You are really not supposed to use the lightweight one for chopping bones, but I chop chicken bones with it. If a nick appears, I just sharpen the blade and proceed. I like the cleaver for slicing icebox cookies, making cole slaw, scooping vegetables and meat after slicing, chopping foods, using the handle for a pestle to smash seasonings, cutting watermelons and pounding like a mallet with the blade. I favor it even for Japanese cookery.

One lady keeps hers beside her when she is alone at home. Wow! She is prepared to scare away any intruder. It does look that vicious!

One wonders how such a knife could be so convenient—so versatile. The blade is about 4 inches wide and 8 inches long. With two cleavers you can mince simultaneously any meat or vegetable without the loss of juices, a far better method than grinding the meat which smashes the pieces as it is forced through the grinder blade.

WOK—AN ANCIENT COOKING PAN

The *wok* is a special Chinese spherical salad-bowl-shaped pan. It is an invention that has basically remained the same through the ages. Originally, it was designed to fit over a clay brick mound with wood burning below and a hole at the top to support the *wok*. It is at its best in heavy rolled steel (not stainless) with a ring adapter stand and cover. A set like this sells for about ten dollars. I would advise you not to buy a light weight type at discount stores or ones that are advertised in mail order catalogs at a few dollars. You will be greatly disappointed—the heat retention will be poor and they are light and shallow; a sad imitation of the true, heavy steel *wok*. The 14-inch size is ideal for general home use since this will permit you to use all the stove burners at the same time. I often use my small 12-inch one for breakfast. I put bacon slices around the edges and the fat dribbles into the center. Then, after the bacon is semi-crisp, I drain most of the oil and put my egg in the center. Cover and cook over medium-low heat and lo!—I have the nicest fried egg sunnyside up with a soft cloudy film over the yolk!

Always heat the *wok* very hot, then add oil and when it is sizzling, splash the oil all over the surfaces of the *wok* with your spatula. You are now ready to start toss-frying fast! It is also unsurpassed for deep-fat frying. There is little spatter because of the high sides. You can use it over gas (the ideal heat source), electric or on an outdoor fire unit.

I do not care for the stainless steel *woks* since heat retention is poor and food does not cook rapidly enough nor does it brown very well either. It does not rust like the plain steel ones do on occasion, but then it costs much more without having many advantages. So why not buy an authentic *wok* and save money?

Do not leave foods in your *wok* after you are finished cooking. Remove to a serving dish as soon as the cooking is finished. The heat retention is excellent but like the old time black cast iron skillets, food should be removed because there will be a metallic flavor transfer.

The *wok* can be used as a steamer. You can cook soup, spaghetti sauce, make stew and just about anything with one pan! Spectacular!

WOK SPATULA

There is a special iron Chinese spatula for the *wok* that fits the curvature of the pan edge. It is very crudely made by hand and sells for under seventy-five cents but it is extremely functional. As you cook and toss-fry your foods, there is no bowl of the usual spoon to delay your cooking process. All the ingredients just slip off the flat surface of the spatula—makes for speedy cooking!

JAPANESE GRATER

A small metal or ceramic one is indispensable. I use it for ginger, *daikon* (radish), and citrus grating often. I even keep one small ceramic one with a chunk of ginger on it in my refrigerator. It's always there when I need it. You should try it!

RICE COOKER

An electric Japanese rice cooker is automatic and costs about twenty dollars for a 5-cup American measurement size (a smaller one costs less, occasionally as low as fourteen dollars). If you consider buying a toaster or waffle iron it is not any different cost-wise, but the waffle iron, especially if you use it only once in awhile costs more in the end. One could use the rice cooker easily three or four times a week.

Rice is always cooked uniformly in the electric cooker. Every grain is perfect. You will have no more burnt rice, although crisp browned rice has a special flavor that is delicious. This is a wonderful pan for making *pilaf*. For busy mothers having children at ball practice, music lessons, and so on, this cooker is a life saver. Get your rice ready to go in the pan, push the button which automatically cooks the rice grains to perfection—get in the automobile to tend to your car pool duties—when you come home the rice is ready. If you had also prepared in advance your ingredients for a quick Oriental dish, you can now whip up a fabulous entree in minutes after you enter the house.

JAPANESE RICE PADDLE

This rice paddle (*samoji*) is a convenient wooden tool used for serving rice and comparable to our versatile rubber spatula or wooden spoon. Wet the *samoji* with water so the rice kernels will not stick. Fluff up the hot rice loosely before serving. Do not mash. This paddle works well to serve mashed potatoes or even ice cream. The large size paddle is outstanding for cookie making as compared to a wooden spoon—the spoon has a concave hollow bowl and materials lodge there. The paddle is flat and scrapes off nicely at the edge of the bowl. You'll discover more spectacular uses. The tool is only twenty-five cents. In ceramics class I have even seen a person spanking the clay with this type of paddle. It might come in handy for disciplining kids, too!

CHOPSTICKS

I prefer the long Chinese bamboo type chopsticks for all cooking. They are very inexpensive and very sturdy. It's glorious to fry bacon with chopsticks. You can pick the pieces and flip them and let go in seconds! For eating either Chinese or Japanese foods, I prefer the Japanese bamboo chopsticks that come in individual paper wrappings. There are two kinds, one made from plain wood and the other from bamboo. The wooden kind is very inexpensive but breaks easily. The bamboo ones are very solid in feel and for economy they can be used over again after washing. There are ivory and lacquered as well as newer plastic chopsticks, but food does have a tendency to slide off. For utility and practical purposes the bamboo chopsticks do the trick! They constitute the most satisfactory way to cook or eat that I know. Try them and see if you don't agree with me. Even at a picnic you could always find a few twigs and devise your own set.

CHINESE BRASS WIRE SKIMMER

This skimmer comes in many sizes from about 4 inches to 12 inches in diameter. It is unequalled for removing big chunks of food or whole chickens from deep-fat, meats from a stew pot and the like. One lady told me that for two generations, her family used this skimmer in the garden by the fish pond for catching the goldfish when cleaning the pond water was necessary—while in one of my classes she discovered what it is really used for—cooking! It has a heavy, long bamboo handle and the wires form an open weave much like chicken wire.

JAPANESE TEMPURA STRAINER

This strainer is most useful for removing the darkened particles from deep-fat frying. I even use it as a strainer when pouring out liquids from a pan. It is inexpensive and most convenient. The strainer is a wire mesh about 3 inches in diameter.

The aforementioned tools and utensils are basics but one can still use a skillet or a Dutch oven or whatever you have in your cupboard. If you were going to buy just the minimum for convenience, I would suggest the *wok*, the cleaver, the spatula for the *wok* and the rice cooker (a little luxury but worth the investment).

MANNERS: TRADITIONAL? MODERN? WHAT IS THE APPROACH?

Festive, friendly, and flavorsome good eating would be the most descriptive words one could use for Oriental meals. Chinese-style, a variety of community entrees are placed in the center and a bowl of rice is at each place with a small plate for your various food servings. Everyone eats small helpings from the common serving bowls. Japanese-style, traditionally, has the servings placed nicely (very small quantities of food) and so artistically on many little dishes and bowls. And to follow the best of etiquette one would flip over the chopsticks and use the top, the blunt ends, to serve oneself from any central serving bowl if there was such an entree. You would eat with the pointed tips only. This would be especially true as in the case of *sukiyaki* and *shabu-shabu nabe* dishes. For practical Western-style family use, one large dinner plate will do. In fact in America, with everyone so active and most of us eating in shifts, we couldn't even begin to adapt the fine points of Oriental etiquette for our daily living. But it is nice to know how the native Japanese enjoy a tranquil meal time.

If chopsticks are inconvenient for you, use your fork and spoon. I've heard the remark that chopsticks are fine but so time consuming to use. I must admit forks do pick up food in quantities more conveniently, especially when you are desperately hungry. But remember, in the Oriental manner of eating to lift the rice bowl or soup bowl in your hand is permissible. This is why chopsticks work well, you have a bowl of hot, steaming rice to back up any spills, etc.

You can serve tea without a saucer. There are certain "holds," though, that are more dignified than others. You can make all kinds of slurpy noises drinking soup or noodles and it is considered good etiquette. Also, it is considered ill manners to leave as much as a grain of rice in your bowl.

I do believe the mug serving of soups in America is wonderful and so practical. You have to bring it up to your mouth and none of it spills. However, the lovely soups of Japanese cuisine cannot quite be appreciated in a mug—the clear soup graced with the bits of yellow lemon peel, the one curled pink shrimp and the touch of green vegetable in a red lacquered bowl—it is too exquisite. One must enjoy it partially with his eyes! In genuine classic Japanese cuisine a part of the true enjoyment of gracious dining is the feeling of *shibui*—that certain serenity and depth of meaning to everything—so subtle and so elegant and so delicate. We Americans could all probably benefit from a bit of this feeling. However, be practical for your own convenience. Why be a slave to traditions if you can get along and devise some shortcuts? There is a time and a place for both. We in America can do as we wish and use the dignified manners that we grew up with. When you are in the Orient you can follow tradition as they do.

The one custom that I dearly love, observed by both the Chinese and the Japanese, is to serve a hot, steaming rolled up hand towel, often perfumed, both before and after a meal. It is elegant to feel so clean. Try it! We could nicely adapt this "manner" at our meals.

ENTERTAINING ASIAN STYLE FOR AMERICANS

The cheery greetings, the exchange of words of old-time friends, the display of your genuine hospitality is often cramped at parties, but with Oriental food you can plan some of the dishes that will give you time to visit. Using a "cook yourself" menu, you can be a guest (almost) at your own party. Use electric skillets, *hibachi*, or even the new butane gas burning stoves or to be truly informal, you could use the fireplace in the winter months. Your home, be it in the dining room, the kitchen, the patio or the family room can be a place to serve these foods. There is a warmth and a graciousness that you cannot achieve in a restaurant. Somehow, Oriental foods dictate the more informal settings so ideally suited to our casual American living habits.

Consider at a Japanese dinner party that there is no concept of matched dinner sets. It is not the food that is the most outstanding (it sometimes has a tendency to disappoint the uninitiated)—the charm and the beautiful artistic variety is what is so appealing. The multiplicity of designs, colors, and shapes of the porcelain, the pottery and the lacquer ware is fantastic.

The astonishing array and number of little dishes would fill our dishwashers! Each plate has its own identity—none of this one pattern, one material and one shape conformity to a certain style. There is a certain humble richness to what would otherwise be a dull routine—an artistry that identifies our human desire to express ourselves as individuals.

SOME PARTY STYLES

A devoted student planned a party having recipes all set up and his ingredients prepared in advance with recipes attached.

Each invited guest as well as the host followed his written recipe and did his "thing" with electric skillets, *woks* and deep-fryers in the kitchen and on the patio. Within a very brief time the meal was whipped up before people could be bored! Cocktails were being imbibed at the same time and the zest with which everyone proceeded to try it must have been fantastic! No doubt some drinks disappeared into some of the Oriental concoctions, too. They had a wonderful time, so I was told.

My friend, a vivacious French lady, planned a party for several weeks. Every chance she had, she cooked and sliced meat and so forth, froze whatever she could, and on the eventful day of the party for fourteen persons, she served nine courses, plus her rice, tea and dessert. Her guests all signed a scroll declaring her "a very excellent Oriental cook" and stating that she had passed the gourmets' taste test with flying colors. She brought to class the ornate signed paper, all decorated and attached with miniature flags of the Orient and one of the United States, as well as bells and ribbons dangling. What love, imagination and gaiety went into the preparation of that party to make it such a success!

As told in Ecclesiastes, for everything there is a season and a time for every matter under heaven—a time to be born, a time to die, a time to plant and so on. Now seems to be the right time for Oriental cooking with the tremendous surge of interest, the astonishing curiosity of the inquisitive Americans for Oriental foods. Everyone is cooking—some good—some bad.

Much of the pseudo-type of Oriental cooking is terrible. Once the real, subtle flavors have been discovered, you will understand the terrific appeal that exists for Asian cooking. If you invite someone to dine out, over half of the time the answer is: "How about some Oriental food?"

We can, in our American style, do a Japanese-style meal with fabulous success. For the steak dinner *teppan-yaki,* have a tray on a small table near the host or the hostess. All food should be pre-cut in the kitchen and arranged neatly on colorful platters before the actual cooking starts.

To prepare any of these at-the-table-meals, all you have to

provide each diner is a bowl of rice, dipping sauces and a salad or two. The guests will be helping themselves to the foods as they get cooked on your electric skillet.

This is a friendly and festive way to entertain and easy on the hostess. Of course, if you sit on soft cushions at a coffee table Japanese-style with your shoes off, and perhaps a Japanese kimono on, the atmosphere would be elegant—even if the sitting at the floor level produces leg cramps! It certainly gives one a relaxed, friendly feeling. I do believe Japanese-style cooking offers one of the warmest, most hospitable ways to entertain. Through partaking of food together people all over the world could understand each other better and the international peace of the world could certainly be resolved!

The Japanese, especially, are great ones for entertaining to conduct business. One of my relatives, who is of the top echelon in Tokyo, tells me that if you do not partake of drinks and dining with your business contacts, you get nowhere in Japan. Partying and expense account entertaining is very much a part of Japanese business philosophy. A great deal of friendly drinking accompanies these festive parties, and one is not criticized if he imbibes a bit too much and the next day can't remember what he said.

HOW-TO SECTION

HOW TO USE CHOPSTICKS

Chopsticks are easy to manipulate. How? Rest one stick at the base of the thumb and the other end near the tip of the ring finger. The thumb firmly holds this stick immobile. The other stick is held as if you were writing with a pencil. The third finger supports and lifts the stick. It does all the work of moving up and down. The stick tips must be even. Tap on the table gently if there is need to check on this evenness. Hold about one-third way down from top for good leverage. As in many manually operated tools, there will be all kinds of variations. No matter how you hold the chopsticks, if it serves the purpose successfully, that is the important factor. You can grip objects like meat but lift elusive foods like noodles by sliding under and scooping up. I have even seen people spear foods when they couldn't hold them properly. Such use is not the best of chopstick etiquette, however.

You will discover, once you have the technique mastered, chopsticks are invaluable for whisking, for turning, for mixing your ingredients, for cooking and above all for eating! They can be used for a knife, by holding one stick in each hand and making a criss-cross action with them on the piece of food that you wish to split in half. It works—try it! If necessary it is not considered improper to lift the piece up to your mouth with your chopsticks. It is permissible to take a nibble and replace the morsel back on the dish.

I am inclined to think chopstick use is an advancement over the fork because I find it has more uses. Frying bacon is a snap, removing a pickle lodged deep in the jar, retrieving dropped items—all are so speedy with chopsticks. I even use one very long thin one for turning a tubing when I am doing some home sewing. I can operate faster with chopsticks. In Chinese, the character for chopsticks literally means "quick ones." You'll agree with me once you are skillful in manipulating them.

HOW TO TOAST SESAME SEEDS

Use a heavy bottomed skillet to "toast" seeds. Heat pan, using no oil. Add seeds and keep shaking like popcorn, just a few minutes. The natural oil from the seeds will come out slightly to prevent any sticking. Watch carefully since they do burn very easily.

For certain Japanese dishes, we can crush the seeds in a *suribachi,* literally translated as a rubbing bowl. The inside of this interesting clay pot is coarsely serrated like a comb run through wet clay. A special stick or *bo* is part of the set. Put in your toasted seeds and start crushing by a circular motion of the stick, actually a mortar and pestle action. You can substitute for this bowl and stick by using an electric blender but, occasionally, some authenticity of tools makes the gourmet cooks even more inspired. And, with compliments flying, one has a tendency to keep improving and getting more authentic!

Another way to crush the seeds is between two pieces of waxpaper. Use a rolling pin for the smashing job. Commercially packaged (imported) toasted seeds just are not satisfactory, they seem to have a sort of staleness even if the containers are vacuum sealed.

The heavenly aroma of crushed sesame seeds is exquisite and one that you will always savour. Someone told me it was as good as sniffing steak to them! I wonder about that. I would rather have a real steak. An appreciation of the delectable aroma of ground sesame seeds as well as the visual beauty of the food being prepared is just as important as knowing your Oriental ingredients. Somehow, this knowledge of the natural and aesthetic beauty fulfills a need for the Japanese traditionalist.

A most unusual use for sesame seeds (stale or fresh ones or even buggy ones!) is to make small pin cushions of them! The oil from the seeds prevents rust in pins and needles and the pins couldn't care less if the seeds are old or not. The Orientals are ingenious!

HOW TO KEEP MUSHROOMS FRESH

Select the choicest, clean, solid, unopened caps of mushrooms at the produce market. Avoid the bruised and discolored ones. I always reach for a paper bag and not the plastic ones to store my mushrooms. In a brown paper bag with the top left open, the unwashed fungi will keep for days in excellent condition in the refrigerator. I never put them in the vegetable crisper of the refrigerator since this causes sweating and a slimy condition. The sealed plastic bag has the same effect on the mushrooms. Very quickly rinse off any sediment on the mushrooms under the cold water tap just before you are ready to use them. Do not soak in water since the absorption of moisture is rapid with mushrooms.

Mushrooms can be frozen whole. Do not wash. Simply put them in an air-tight container and place in the freezer. When ready to use, thaw and quickly rinse. If you should want to dehydrate some fresh mushrooms, this is a simple process. String mushrooms with a needle and heavy thread and hang them in the sun to dry out quickly or put them in a very low (150°F.) oven. Watch carefully. You can keep the dried mushrooms in a plastic bag in the refrigerator or store them in the freezer. This prevents infestation with bugs. This is a good way to store any dried fruits, like raisins, apricots, peaches, prunes or whatever.

HOW TO STRAIN OIL AFTER DEEP-FAT FRYING

Place a funnel in the neck of an empty bottle. Use a double layer of heavy 2-ply paper towels. (You'll have to try different brands. Some are thin and some are thicker. There are several brands on the retail market which are quite sturdy and do not tear.) Fold papers together as one, in half, then into quarters. Use one section of the quartered paper as a filter lining the funnel. Pour in the used oil. This will clarify the used oil beautifully, perhaps with a slight bit of color change. Strained oil can be refrigerated and used over again.

If there is a lot of color alteration (darkened) I would prefer to discard the used oil instead of using it again since a chemical change has occurred. To prevent such changes, keep your heat under the oil controlled carefully. Medium high is the best for deep-fat frying—about 350° to 375°F. Some people use old oil plus new to fry, but actually it is a shame to spoil new oil by adding old. However, much depends upon how long the old oil was heated and used. Use your common sense about whether to add new to old or whether to just toss it out.

I use this same paper towel filter method, for filtering my coffee grounds to make my breakfast drip-method coffee and have no more need to buy fancy filter papers.

ORIENTAL ENVELOPE WRAP

This method of wrapping or enclosing things is sometimes referred to in America as a diaper fold. This envelope wrap method is used all over the Orient—in homes, in department stores, as a way of enclosing food portions like egg rolls, chicken in papers, and beef in parchment. It saves string, makes for a wasteless way to use paper and is terrifically versatile. You will probably think up some other valid reasons for yourself. I believe it is artistic, too. Try wrapping your gift packages this way. You will use less paper.

Place the square of paper, cloth or noodle paste skin (like *won ton* skin and egg roll skin) in front of you like a diamond. Fold the bottom corner up to the center, a wee bit past the center point. Next fold the left and then the right corners over toward the center. Lastly, fold down the top corner to the bottom of the packet. Give it a tuck into the bottom edge to secure it between the first and the two side folds. Another way would be to bring that last corner toward the bottom and glue it into place around the bottom edge with glue or egg, as the case may be.

The Japanese have a most delightful way to carry small items. They wrap small objects such as books in a scarf (*furoshiki*). Place your items in the center, bring the opposite sides of the scarf to the center and tie a knot. Repeat for the other sides, making a double knot for security. And there you have a handy modern "tote" bag!

A QUICK AND EASY METHOD TO CLEAN SHRIMPS

To remove shrimp shell from the underside where the legs are, insert your thumb under the peel of the shrimp and with a slight peeling action remove the shell. If your recipe calls for the tails to be left on, at the part where the tail meets the shell break off. You can also leave about ¼ inch of the shell on the body proper to support the tail. Leaving the tails on, especially for *tempura,* gives the cook a handle with which to dip in the batter besides a good, reddish tint in contrast to the golden-pinkish shade of the batter when it is fried.

To clean the veins, put paper towels on board, place shrimp flat on papers and insert the cleaver at the back edge. Slice partially into the shrimp back and with a dragging outward motion

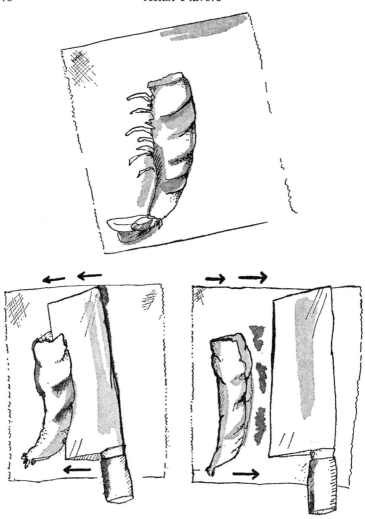

to the right of the cleaver remove the vein onto the towel. This method surely beats holding a shrimp in the hands and trying to work the vein out. Some persons tediously use a toothpick or a small knife to remove the dark lines. With my technique, a pound of shrimps can be deveined in minutes. After finishing the job of vein removal, just discard the paper. Rinse and dry shrimps and proceed with your recipe. If you desire to leave the shells on the shrimps and wish to devein, do it in the same manner described, cutting right through the shell. Use an especially sharp knife or cleaver to do the job easily. Actually, sometimes the shrimps are not highly veined and you can cook them without going through this tedious step. The non-removal will not be that noticeable in the final dish. Some people never devein shrimp even with heavy veins.

TRY GROWING ORIENTAL VEGETABLES FROM SEED

Growing vegetables from seed is not as difficult as you might imagine—no different from any other vegetable garden you may have tried growing in the past. Here is a list of some of the varieties you might try.

Yard-long beans
Bok choy (Chinese chard)
Mustard greens
Nappa cabbage
Japanese cucumbers, very similar to Armenian and Italian types
Japanese eggplants
Garland chrysanthemum (edible leaves for *tempura,* soups and so on)
Edible pod peas
Icicle radish (*daikon*)
Burdock (*gobo*)
Chinese parsley (coriander)
Matrimonial vine (*gau gay*)
Bitter melon
Taro (Japanese potato), sometimes referred to as elephant's ear plant

The main difficulty in growing such vegetables would be a source of seed supply. The large Chinatown stores may be able to give you leads, your nursery man may know, or you may have an Oriental friend or two who could suggest places to buy these seeds. There are companies that specialize in unusual seeds throughout the country.

A very fresh ginger root often grows nicely in a pot in the house—try it the next time you get a solid one with perhaps an "eye" ready to grow.

HOW TO GROW BEAN SPROUTS
HOW TO CLEAN BEAN SPROUTS
WHAT ABOUT CANNED BEAN SPROUTS?

Even if you live in the remotest section of the country, if you can order some dried mung beans, you can grow and eat an Oriental vegetable by following these simple directions.

Soak 1 cup dried mung beans (sold in 1 lb. packages) overnight in lukewarm water. They will double in size. One-half cup dried mung beans yields about 1 lb. fresh bean sprouts. Place

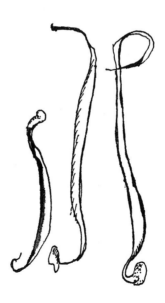

several layers of clean cheesecloth in a colander or a clean pan with some drainage holes punched out at the bottom. Put in the soaked beans. Cover with a double layer of cheesecloth. Water with lukewarm water. Drain. Keep in a dark place like an oven or a closet. Temperature, ideally, should be about 70°F. Water your beans very carefully every 4 to 5 hours except at night. Always drain well. Keep up this watering process daily.

In 4 to 5 days the sprouts can be harvested when about 1 to 1½ inches long. They may even be ready in 3 days.

Put the entire crop into a large basin filled with cold water. Swirl the waters and the sprouts around. Most of the sprouts will fall to the bottom. Drain well, removing any greyish-green hulls that may be floating at the surface. Pack in plastic bags and keep them in the refrigerator. Remember bean sprouts do not freeze well. They lose that crunchiness that is so appealing about them. Never substitute for the fresh bean sprouts by using canned ones, which are poor in flavor and add nothing to the texture of the dish. Omit them instead. A similar texture can be achieved by slicing lettuce or cabbage in thin shreds; personally, if I do not have any bean sprouts, I leave them out. When shopping look for creamy white, crisp mung bean sprouts. If they have begun to turn brown or slimy do without. Generally, bean sprouts are fairly clean when purchased, with no grey-green hulls, etc. The easiest, quickest and most practical method to wash your fresh sprouts is to put them in a large plastic bag. Fill with cold water. Jerk the bag up and down a few times. Then stab a few holes at the bottom of the ballooned out bag and you have an automatic strainer. No extra colander to wash and your cleaning job of the bean sprouts is finished!

Try versatile fresh bean sprouts in salads and as a fried vegetable (Americanized). The fastidious cook trims the stringy roots and even the heads of fresh mung bean sprouts but I do not bother since they are all edible parts.

Tossed Salad With Bean Sprouts

Blanch sprouts in hot water for 1 minute to remove that raw taste. Drain. Run through cold water to cut the cooking process. Marinate in your favorite salad dressing. Then add your crackly fresh greens and toss just before serving. You could add sliced tomatoes or cucumbers, if you like.

Fried Bean Sprouts

Bean sprouts fried in butter for 2 minutes with salt, pepper and a dash of MSG are excellent with steaks or chops as a vegetable. Combine with fresh mushrooms or edible-pod peas and cook ever so briefly. You could substitute pieces of cut-up bacon for the butter. Fry and drain part of the oil and proceed as above. Just a dash of soy goes well with this, too. Do not substitute canned bean sprouts. There is absolutely no similarity in taste or texture.

HOW TO FRY RICE STICKS, RICE NOODLES, KAKIMOCHI AND SHRIMP FLAVORED CHIPS

Rice Sticks—Mai Fun

The rice sticks (*mai fun*) we use for chicken salads and for "Snow Over the Mountain" as well as other Chinese recipes. It is like a vermicelli made with rice. Some packages of *mai fun* come like a wiry batch of shredded wheat and others come packed in small bunches about 1 inch in diameter and 5 inches long, tied together neatly. Then again you may find some which are in tiny, tiny bundles about 1 inch long and tied together. If you go to a very well stocked market such as those in Chinatown you will find as many as 8 or 10 different kinds. Many have the same wrappings but the Chinese characters are varied. So ask the clerks and if they are not able to assist you, do the best you can to guess which package is the one you should buy. They all will work more or less. The long bundles 5 inches or so long and tied together are my favorites.

They are tricky to prepare at first, but once you learn how to do it, you begin to wonder why you were afraid to try in the first place. Untie and loosely spread out the long strands of rice sticks. Grasp a small quantity at a time and deep-fry in lots of hot oil (350°F.). These puff up instantly. Flip them over and

quickly drain on paper towels. They can be prepared hours ahead of time.

Rice Noodles—Sha Ho Fun

One of the favorites of the students is *sha-ho* rice sticks or rice noodles, petite 1½-inch by 1 inch by ¼-inch rolls of noodles. The sticks are made from rice flour and water, then dehydrated. These can be boiled and you can use your favorite sauces (Oriental, European or American) or do as I love to do—break the rolls into 1-inch long strands and deep-fry in vegetable oil. They burst up in seconds into fabulous curls. Immediately remove while still white. Drain on paper towels. Place in a bowl and sprinkle with salt, or use some favorite flavorings of your own. Some people use Parmesan grated cheese, salad dressing powdered mixes and so on. Serve like potato chips as a snack.

Kakimochi Rice (glutinous) Chips (Japanese)

These come in sesame, seaweed, shrimp and sweet flavors, usually mixed up in one package. They expand in hot oil just like the rice sticks. *Kakimochi* is an easy-to-do snack and comes packaged in plastic bags. They have a sweeter taste than the rice sticks, which are flavorless except for the seasonings you put on.

Shrimp Flavored Chips (Indonesian)

Shrimp flavored chips made from tapioca flour and shrimps are Indonesian in origin but most of the chips we buy commercially in boxes are produced in Hong Kong. The chips come in various colors. Deep-fry a few at a time at about 375° F. Test one chip first. It should puff up almost instantly. Drain. These fried chips can be used as a garnish, or can be served like potato chips and go especially well with drinks. They are already salted and flavored. Often, fried shrimp or chicken is placed on a prepared white, crispy shrimp chip and the dish is given a fancy name like "chicken on a cloud."

All of the above make instant *hors d'oeuvres* or TV snacks.

Many mothers in my classes have taught the above items to their Brownie, Blue Bird and Cub Scout groups. The kids feel this is fantastic to see the food items explode and grow with such speed and turn out so perfectly each time—a lot different from popcorn which everyone already knows! These strange Oriental food stuffs are different and taste elegant. Try them! They are so simple to do.

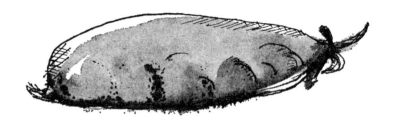

HORS D'OEUVRES

Here are some appetizers and *hors d'oeuvres* which could be used with cocktails, as late-supper snacks, as part of a tea or wedding reception, open house, or as just plain nibbling! There are many, many others in the stores for you to try as well—search for them!

Many have recipes in this book, using some Oriental ingredients adapted for use in America—or anywhere in the world. The remaining items can be purchased ready to use either in cans, in the store freezer compartments, or as fresh items, as the case may be.

Fresh *kamaboko* (steamed fishcake), sliced

Fried, fresh fish *tempura*, available in your Oriental food delicatessen

Slices of eel *kabayaki*—a sort of *teriyaki* packed in cans

Dried strips of octopus or cuttlefish, seasoned with soy and sugar

Canned fish cakes *(tempura)* like a croquette

Japanese rice flour crackers (not so sweet—*arare*), soy flavored

Assorted Oriental pickles

   Beni shoga—preserved Japanese red-colored ginger

   Sweet mixed ginger—assorted vegetables pickled on the sweet side

   Rakkyo—delicious pickled sweet scallions (very popular with Westerners)

   Tokyozuke—assorted Oriental vegetables pickled with sugar and soy

Smoked seafoods: salmon, oysters, clams and fish

Seafoods: *hokki* clams (the size of silver dollars), eel, sauries, abalone, and so many different varieties waiting to be discovered by you

Baby abalone (canned) on sticks, flavored with soy and sugar

Squares of *aji tsuke nori*—seasoned seaweed

Assorted fruits, fresh, canned or preserved types

Salted, licorice flavored preserved plums

Fresh lichee

Baby seasoned abalone on half shells

Candied coconut

Fortune cookies as well as selections of various shapes and flavors in Oriental rice cookies

Almond and sesame cookies

Licorice flavored ginger (red-color)

Dry fried shrimps

Abalone (canned) cubed, use a dip of lemon juice, soy and MSG

Rolled beef *hors d'oeuvres*

Chicken or beef *teriyaki* speared on sticks

Sashimi with a bit of *daikon* slice or lettuce could be rolled and speared on a pick with dip of soy and grated ginger

Small size *sushi*—fish, egg, *nori* (seaweed), etc.

Kakimochi crackers

Shrimp chips

Slices of *char siu*—this is popular any time, any place—make plenty

Rice noodles *(sha-ho* rice sticks), deep-fried, salted or sprinkled with Parmesan cheese or a salad dressing mix powder

Tea eggs

Plum blossom eggs

Japanese egg roll

Japanese salad sauces as dips for raw vegetables

Tempura made up in small pieces

Chicken in papers

Beef in parchment

Won ton (fried) with sweet and sour dip sauce

Egg rolls (Chinese)

Vegetables cooked with meat Japanese *nishime,* served cold
Five spice chicken livers and gizzards
Sui mai

There are endless variations from the regular recipes in this book that you could adapt to appetizer servings by making the portions small and easy to pick up. You will be inventing your own combinations soon.

FANCIFUL APPETIZERS

Sausage Filling (Americanized)

Use "brown and serve" sausages cut into pieces and wrapped in *won ton* skins. Fold into triangle. Seal the edges with egg and deep-fry. Serve hot.

Crab Filling (Americanized)

1 cup crab meat, remove cartilages	1 green onion, chopped
	dash of MSG
3 oz. pkg. cream cheese	¼ tsp. salt
	dash of pepper

Blend all together. Put a small quantity in *won ton* skin. Fold into a triangle. Seal edges with egg and deep-fry. Serve hot.

Chinese Candy With Won Ton Skins

⅓ cup angel flake coconut	⅓ cup brown sugar
⅓ cup chopped peanuts	

Mix all together. Put 1 tsp. mixture into each *won ton* square. Fold into triangle. Seal edges really well with beaten egg. Be sure to press down firmly. Otherwise, there will be a tendency for sugar to ooze out during the frying process. Deep-fry at 375° F. until golden brown. The *won tons* puff up like miniature cushions. Drain on paper towels. Cool and put in air-tight container. Keeps nicely if you can hide it in some unknown cupboard. These are similar to peanut-brittle inside. This sweet *won ton* can be very nicely added to any buffet along with the regular meat *won tons.* Just make sure people know which is the candy type and do not start dunking in sweet and sour sauce. There are endless varieties of sweet fillings using dates, sesame seeds, corn syrup, walnuts, etc. You could even devise some concoctions of your own. It is a fun way to experiment. I have found the children love to make these.

Edible-Pod Pea Appetizers

Scald edible-pod peas for 1 minute in hot water. Dash them under cold water to cut the cooking process. Open the side without the immature pea carefully. Fill this opening with your favorite cream cheese canapè spread for a very different nibble!

Rolled Beef Hors d'Oeuvres

Take thin slices of tender beef, such as *sukiyaki* meat, and roll cigarette style. Wrap a slightly parboiled green onion top around the meat. Tie a knot or fasten with toothpicks. Marinate in your favorite *teriyaki* sauce. Broil for about 5 minutes, turning once, on the *hibachi* or in the broiler of your oven. Be sure to preheat broiler before starting. Fillet, top sirloin, or rib eye could be substituted.

Sesame Chicken

3 chicken breasts, cut into bite-sizes	1 Tbsp. sesame oil
	1 clove garlic, crushed
4 Tbsp. sherry	1 tsp. grated ginger
5 Tbsp. soy	5 Tbsp. toasted sesame seeds
4 Tbsp. sugar	

Combine sherry, soy, sugar, oil, garlic and ginger with the chicken pieces. MSG could be added in dashes, if desired. Marinate 30 minutes or longer. Drain. Skewer on sticks. Broil 4 to 5 minutes until browned. Dip in toasted sesame seeds. Serve hot or cold.

Fresh Bean Curd Cakes

Cut the bean curd cakes *(tofu)* into small cubes. Use a dip of soy and bits of dried bonito flakes *(katsuobushi)* sprinkled on top.

Roasted Soy Beans (similar to salted nuts)

1 cup dried soy beans	3 Tbsp. oil
water	salt to taste

Wash beans and put in large bowl. Cover with water about 1 inch above the level of the beans. Soak overnight. Drain. Rub with a cloth and spread out on a tray to dry. When the skins of the beans are dry, spread on a cookie sheet. Sprinkle with oil and shake in order to coat the beans evenly. Preheat oven to 350° F. and place beans on middle shelf. Roast until brown, about 45 minutes. Shake and stir beans often. Sprinkle with salt and serve like any salted nuts. You will be surprised at their crunchy and good flavor! Another method: After soaking and drying, you can deep-fry in oil at 350°F. for 8 to 10 minutes. Drain on paper towels. Sprinkle with salt while still warm.

Miso Dressing Appetizers

For a very practical American usage for *miso* dressing, place all kinds of vegetables, both raw and slightly parboiled, and seafoods like crab legs, shelled, parboiled shrimps, clams, abalone or whatever you desire, in a circular wheel spoke manner on a large round platter. In the center, put the *miso* sauce in a dipping bowl. Have a bundle of wooden skewers in a holder near the platter. Everyone can spear his vegetable and dip into the sauce as he desires.

Some wooden skewers are available with little fortunes attached at the ends, making for interesting conversation. This diversion of reading the fortunes might *slow down* some of the consumption!

There are also available in the import shops little *hors d'oeuvre* two-tine forks that are quite handsome for this sort of use.

DRESSING FOR DIP:

5 Tbsp. *miso* (Japanese white soy bean paste—*shinshu* type is most delicate)	4 Tbsp. rice wine vinegar ½ tsp. MSG 4 Tbsp. sugar

Cream white *miso* in blender. Add remaining ingredients. Mix well.

Daybreak Oranges (Japanese)

Select and wash a good-shaped orange with even bright coloring. Remove a slice from both ends. Cut in half. Slice into ¼-inch semi-circles crosswise. Arrange the slices in attractive overlapping manner. To eat, pick up with fingers and carefully pull the orange pieces apart at peel edges. They will break at the segmented parts. These make a nice garnish or an addition to a buffet table.

Sweet Potato Chips (Filipino)

3 cups thinly sliced sweet potatoes	ice water
	powdered sugar

A special Japanese vegetable shredder with razor sharp blades really makes easy work of paper-thin slicing. Soak the sheer slices of sweet potatoes in ice water for 15 minutes. Dry between paper towels. Heat deep-fat to 350°F. Fry until golden. Drain on paper towels. Sprinkle with powdered sugar. Makes a good snack. Try salt sometimes, too, instead of the powdered sugar.

DIEM SUM (CHINESE)

Diem sum (Chinese filled pastries) is rather like our blue plate special—but much nicer. It is difficult to categorize *diem sum,* they are like appetizers and yet far different from our Western-style canapès. *Diem sum* is loosely translated as "have all your heart desires" . . . "touch of the heart" . . . "gem of the heart" . . . and when you find the delicious morsels in the heart of a good pastry dough, you will agree! You will want to try many kinds and lots of them—they are that good.

This special cuisine offers an endless variety of out of this world taste sensations. Shrimp and pork dumplings, Chinese sausage and mushrooms, roast pork in buns, steamed prawns, beef, mushrooms, bean sprouts all wrapped in dough and spicy cakes are but a few variations. Some are deep-fried and some are steamed or baked—the doughs can be rice flour, wheat, glutinous rice flour and yam. From learning all these variations, you will soon be inventing some of your own.

The idea of *diem sum* is marvelous—it can be served for lunch, snacks, or afternoon tea parties and they make grand *hors d'oeuvres*. Plan a theatre party in your kitchen using the guests to help in the preparation. When all are at work with loving care, speed comes to the food production assembly line and before you know it the *diem sum* are cooked and served and devoured! A simple, spontaneous get-together like this can be a long remembered delight.

Diem sum can be purchased in Chinese specialty shops. Some are commercially frozen. And many of these *diem sum* can be nicely frozen at home and brought out for frying, boiling or whatever you desire.

Ask for a "tea lunch" when you want this kind of a snack in a restaurant.

Sui Mai (Chinese)

½ lb. *won ton* skins
1 cup pork, chopped like peas
1 cup shrimps, shelled and deveined, chopped like peas
2 finely chopped green onions
4 water chestnuts, finely chopped

1 tsp. cornstarch
½ tsp. MSG
1½ tsp. soy (adjust to taste)
½ tsp. sesame oil
dash of salt and pepper
½ tsp. grated ginger
dash of sugar

Actually, *sui mai* requires round *won ton* skins but these are much more expensive so use your square type *won ton* skins and if you are finicky about shape, trim the corners with scissors to make circles. (And, for the very thrifty, save the corner clipping remnants for addition to soup like noodles.) Or, be nonchalant and time-saving (although not authentic) and just leave the squares alone. Have little petals on the edges of your *sui mai* dumplings. Make a cup with the *won ton* skins and add 1 tsp. of filling in the center of the dough. Draw up sides by crimping as you go around the dough to form a shallow cup. Keep center part open. With fingers coat each cup with oil on the outside surfaces so that the dough will not stick to the steamer pan or to each other. Take precautions not to get oil inside when you are crimping the skins since this can prevent the skin from sticking and forming the cup. The skin will just flap down in the steaming process if not properly formed and you will probably have a flattened out skin with a miniature meat ball in the center! Arrange *sui mai* one layer deep on plate, leaving space between. Set this plate in the steamer and steam for 15 minutes or until the pork is done. Serve hot with mustard, soy, sesame oil or sesame seeds, toasted. Whatever your dip, use your imagination! This is part of the fun of cooking Oriental-style.

Curry Savories (Chinese)

1 lb. ground, lean beef like sirloin or round steak (or finely minced chicken meat)
1 Tbsp. curry powder or more
1 small onion, minced very fine
dash of sugar
1 Tbsp. soy
salt and pepper to taste
1 Tbsp. sherry
dash MSG
1 clove garlic, minced
1 egg, slightly beaten, for brushing on top

Heat 1 Tbsp. oil in hot pan. Fry meat and onions with all seasonings until cooked. Cool until firm.

Use your favorite pie crust dough (using 2 cups of flour) or a packaged mix. Roll out dough on floured board about ⅛-inch or thinner, if possible. Cut circles 4 inches in diameter. Place 1 tsp. filling on one side of round dough. Put some water on other half edge of round before bringing the fold over to form a half circle. Press on edges with a fork to seal in the meat mixture. Brush top with slightly beaten egg. Bake on ungreased cookie sheet in preheated 425°F. oven for about 15-20 minutes. Cool before storing. These freeze very well. Can be reheated in the oven just before serving. Pastry tip: try using instantized flour when working with doughs. When flouring your bread board, rolling out dough and so on very little instantized flour will adhere to your pastry. I do not care to use it for general cooking, however.

Meat Buns—Bows (Chinese)

Bow, sometimes spelled *bau,* is pronounced bow rhyming with how. In Honolulu, they are called *manapua.* These *bows* can be made with assorted fillings depending upon the cook's tastes. Makes it easy to invent some of your own specialties.

1 lb. pork, chopped, to size of peas or use ½ pork and ½ shrimp, frying separately and mixing later

3 stalks of green onions, chopped

1 cup fresh mushrooms, chopped, or dried Oriental mushrooms, soaked, squeezed dry and chopped

1 cup water chestnuts or bamboo shoots or celery, (or combination) finely chopped to make 1 cup total volume
Chinese parsley, minced

½ tsp. grated ginger
½ clove garlic, minced
¼ tsp. 5-spices
1 Tbsp. sherry
½ tsp. sugar
2 tsp. honey (I like "clover" best)
2 tsp. soy (or more, if desired)
½ tsp. MSG
1 Tbsp. *hoisin* sauce
salt
½ tsp. cornstarch blended with ¼ cup water
3 (1 lb. size) loaves of frozen bread dough or use your own hot roll recipe

Fry the ginger and the garlic with the meat in a hot, oiled frying pan. Drain the oil, if necessary. Add sherry, sugar, honey, soy, MSG, *hoisin* sauce, salt, Chinese parsley, and 5-spice combination. Mix. Add the vegetables. Toss-fry for 3 to 5 minutes. Thicken with the cornstarch blended with the water. Cool the filling. Refrigerate, if you have time.

FILLING VARIATIONS:

1. Chinese sausage *(lop cheong)* washed and steamed for 15 minutes and finely chopped.
2. Roast pork *(char siu)* chopped, plus a little oyster sauce and a bit of liquid for gravy.
3. Chicken in Papers recipe with finely cut-up chicken.
4. Use your imagination for Americanized fillings. Almost any tasty combination of meat that is very moist or bound together with gravy would be good.
5. True Chinese fillings have chunks of pork fat and the fat is saved especially for making meat buns.

Thaw frozen bread dough, following directions on package. Divide three loaves into 48 walnut-sized pieces. A hot roll mix or your favorite yeast roll dough can be used as well. Add a little sugar to the dry ingredients if you want a more authentic sweet Chinese taste. Flatten each ball of dough into a circle like a hamburger patty. Middle should be thicker than the edges. Place 1 or 2 Tbsp. of filling in center and pinch edges together and twist. Place pinched edges down on 2½-inch foil squares. Allow to rise in a warm place until double in size.

A marvelous, unconventional way to make the yeast dough rise. Get you car out in the driveway. Close all windows. And, of course, the day should be a warm one—not snowing or raining. Place your cloth covered rolls on a cookie sheet in the car. The warm rays of the sunshine will help make your car an ideal heat source—no drafts and your buns will rise evenly! Only thing, don't forget and drive off! You may get shoved out of the car by an ever-expanding dough!

Steam method: This is typical Chinese manner of preparation. Have plenty of hot steam generating when you steam your foods. It is this heat that cooks the food. For steaming put the buns with pinched edges upward and flattened to insure good, thick tops on buns. When the round of dough is being pinched into place the tendency is often to pull too much and the top covering becomes thin, and the steamed dough is so thin it can collapse when removed—or, as one woman told me, it looks like a wrinkled old woman's face! What a fate for a meat bun.

Oven method: Americanized version. Follow directions for making buns, roll top of buns in sesame seeds. Put buns on greased cookie sheet. Let rise until double in size. Bake at 375°F. for 15 minutes or until golden brown. Serve hot with dishes of dry mustard blended to a paste with soy or use only plain soy. The *bow* is dipped in this as it is eaten. These freeze very well. I suggest you bake or steam them first, and when you serve them later steam to reheat. Steam only long enough to heat through or they will become soggy.

The tops of the buns could be "marked" with dots of food

coloring as a code. Use one chopstick and dip in coloring. Make one red mark for one kind, two marks for another and so on.

WON TON AND EGG ROLL SKINS

These noodle base skin wrappers are used in many of the Oriental countries—China, Japan, Korea, Vietnam, Phillippines and Indonesia. Basically, egg noodles, *won ton* skins, egg roll skins, *ravioli* and many other related products are one and the same—they are all made from egg, flour and water. The *won ton* wrapper can be used for an amazing number of purposes—in fact, one of my students of Italian descent uses *won ton* skins for her *ravioli* filling and the egg roll skins for *manicotti*. Actually, cooking is universal in many ways, using the same ingredients with flavor variation depending upon the country's cuisine. It is fantastic that despite the distances between countries so many foods have developed along many of the same lines over the centuries. With each method of cooking—be it pan frying, steaming, deep-fat or boiling—there are all kinds of resultant textures and tastes. By preparing the same item several ways at the same time, one can compare the differences positively.

We are fortunate that we can buy our wrappers ready made and do not have to make them from scratch. They can be purchased either fresh or frozen. Both are of good quality if well packaged. They keep about a week in the refrigerator if they are fresh at the store when you buy them (remember, sometimes they may have been in your grocer's delicatessen case for a few days waiting for you).

Even if I do not always follow as I teach, this is a thrifty tip, and maybe you'll be less wasteful than I am at times. If the skins get too dried out, and you are not able to rescue them, enough to be usable, dry them out more and use the skins in pieces as noodles in a clear soup base. Cooking in boiling salted water and then adding to a cup of commercial broth or dehydrated chicken soup is better than wasting them!

HOW TO REVIVE WON TON AND EGG ROLL SKINS

If the *won ton* edges are dried out from storage, to revive, loosen the package wrappings carefully so as not to break the delicate brittle skins even more. Keep the paper on. Place a paper towel that has been dampened and all the excess moisture squeezed out on top of your opened paper package. Place the entire package, plus the damp towel in a large plastic bag. Close plastic bag and put on the shelf of your refrigerator for 1 day. The skins are often as good as new again. So pliable and ready to use in your favorite way. The main thing to remember is to place the purchased skins in a good airtight plastic or foil wrap in the first place when you store them. Freshness can be retained for a long period of time in the freezer. Take out of the freezer carefully and thaw. Use what you need and refreeze the balance for another time, again wrapping well.

Won Ton—A Sort of Chinese Ravioli

Won ton squares are available commercially, sold in Oriental food stores. These store-bought skins are uniform in thickness, often fresh and so pliable. The frozen variety is of excellent quality if well packaged. Keep very well covered while using the skins since they have a tendency to dry out rapidly. If you buy extra for keeping in the freezer be sure you put them into an airtight packaging material. They will keep up to six months or longer with proper storage conditions. You will need about 1⅓ lbs. *won ton* skins for this filling, deep-fried method; for the boiled type about 1 lb. skins will be sufficient.

In case you just cannot secure *won ton* skins here is a recipe for making the dough.

1½ cups flour	1 beaten egg
1 tsp. salt	2 Tbsp. cold water

Sift the flour and the salt into a mixing bowl. Add the egg and cold water. Knead until smooth, place dough in refrigerator covered for 1 hour. Then, place on a floured board and roll paper thin with rolling pin. Dust dough with flour, cut into 3-inch squares and stack. If you do not use them immediately, wrap carefully in foil and place in freezer.

FILLING:

1 cup pork, chopped like hamburger	1 egg
1 cup shrimps, deveined and minced	¼ tsp. MSG
	1½ tsp. soy (adjust to taste)
2 finely chopped green onions	salt and pepper to taste
4 water chestnuts, chopped fine	½ tsp. sesame oil
	½ tsp. grated ginger

Mix all ingredients together and proceed as directed. (Any left-over filling can be frozen or made into a small patty and steamed for about 15 minutes.) Hold square of *won ton* skin on palm of left hand. Place a dab of filling ½ inch from the corner nearest you. Fold this corner over the dough. Roll it once more toward the center of the square. Put a minute dab of filling on the right-hand corner of the skin. Bring the left-hand corner to it. Press down these two corners to make them stick together. Even if there is some piece of meat filling dangling after the sticking process—do not worry, it will get cooked and you won't notice it in the end result. This finished *won ton* will look like a girl with a bandana over her head. You can almost see her smiling at you!

Or do it the very, very easy way. Put a ¼ tsp. dab in the center of the square of dough in the palm of your hand. Crunch *won ton* skin now by closing your hand like a fist. Toss aside onto a tray where you have them lined up ready to fry or freeze or boil. With this very simplified method, one can really deliver quantities rapidly.

Still another alternative: Put a dab on half of one side of the *won ton* skin. Seal with egg on the edges to form a triangle or rectangle as you desire. Fry in deep-fat about 350°F. until golden. Test one piece of skin first in the oil to see if the temperature is correct, the *won ton* skin should puff out nicely, having the graceful look of butterfly wings. If it browns too readily, then add a bit more cold oil at the edge of the pan to reduce the oil temperature. Using a slotted spoon is excellent for lifting the *won tons* from the oil; but the best tool of all is a Chinese brass wire skimmer with its cool bamboo handle. Drain on paper towels. Serve hot, if possible, although cold servings are still quite presentable. See below for various serving suggestions. Sweet and sour sauce for a dip is a great favorite.

Uncooked filled *won tons* can be frozen after being made up. Place on a cookie sheet and leave space between each piece. Freeze. Pack in a plastic container carefully since they are very fragile at this point. You can make them up early in the morning with plastic film placed between the layers. Cover entire tray of ready to use *won tons* with foil and place in the refrigerator. Defrost before frying. You can freeze the fried *won tons*. Cool after frying. Freeze. Thaw out when wanted and warm in oven just before serving. For boiling, there is no need to thaw out first. Just boil longer to make sure the filling is completely cooked.

More optional uses:

Boiled *won tons* can be served plain like raviolis with a dipping sauce of soy and a few drops of sesame oil plus some green onion shreds.

You can use more filling and boil *won tons* in a pot of boiling water. Put about 10 *won tons* in at one time, stir, and boil until they float. Test one and see if it is cooked; if not, simmer another minute or so. Use a skimmer to remove from water and, if making soup, place 4 or 5 in each serving bowl. Pour your hot soup over the cooked *won tons*. Garnish with a spinach leaf or whatever you desire. A word of caution: do not boil *won tons* in your soup base. By boiling separately in a pot of water first, then adding to the soup base, you will prevent the *won tons* from getting "gooey" and falling apart; important after all the precious time you spent trying to figure how to fold them! You can, also, put fried *won tons* in a bowl and pour hot soup over them, for a different texture from the boiled *won tons* in soup.

Crispy Egg Roll (Chinese)

1 cup shrimps, shelled, deveined and cut into small pieces or substitute 1 can shrimp or crab, drained
1 small clove of garlic, minced
½ cup onion rings, cut in half
½ lb. bean sprouts
½ cup fresh mushrooms, sliced, or Oriental dried mushrooms, soaked in water, squeezed dry and sliced thin
½ tsp. grated ginger
1 Tbsp. toasted sesame seeds (optional)
½ cup celery, slashed in layers, then cut in thin 1½-inch strips
1 tsp. salt
dash of MSG
1 Tbsp. soy
¼ tsp. sugar
dash of pepper
1 pkg. of egg roll skins purchased from store. You will need about ½ to ⅔ lb. for this recipe—use what you need and repackage carefully. Freeze remainder of skins.
1 egg, beaten slightly, for sealing edges

Fry shrimps in hot pan with 1 Tbsp. oil, garlic, ginger and salt until pink. Remove from frying pan. (If using canned shellfish, there is no need to pre-fry.) Sauté onions, mushrooms, celery and seasonings. Fry only about 1 or 2 minutes. Keep toss-frying. Remove from pan and add to shrimp. Fry bean sprouts in hot pan for 1 minute and add to shrimp mixture. Toss well together. (If sesame seeds are used, toast first and add last to bean sprouts and mix together.) Allow filling to cool. Refrigerate. Drain in a colander pressing down to remove as much juice as possible. Save this juice to add to soup at some other meal. Keep egg roll skin well covered with wax paper while working so they will not dry out. If dry, refer to the section "How to Revive *Won Ton* and Egg Roll Skins." Place about 3 Tbsp. filling on center of skin. Keep ingredients together—not spread out thinly. Take the corner of the skin nearest you and fold over the filling, like an envelope being made up. Please refer to the section "Oriental Envelope Wrap."

Brush the edges of the skin with beaten egg. Fold both sides toward the center, then roll to close and keep tight. Size will be about 1½ inches in diameter and 4 inches long. I like to make up about 3 at a time, since they cannot stand too long without getting soggy. Often the skin will tear and rips occur. To repair these catastrophes, brush with a little egg and make a patch with a piece of spare egg roll skin.

The rolls can be fried at this point in deep-fat or coated with the following batter first. The batter coating gives a nice crunchiness.

¼ cup dry biscuit mix   6 or 7 Tbsp. ice water
¼ cup cornstarch

Quick dipping and immersing in the hot oil will take some practice to do well. I manage to work with chopsticks, but you may want to use tongs very gently. Deep-fry in about 4 inches of oil at 350°F. Keep turning them until golden brown. They have a tendency to want to stay in one position because an air pocket develops inside the egg roll. They should be fried at least 5 minutes or more to insure cooking of the entire skin, especially, at the corners where there are several layers. Drain on paper towels. To serve, prepare a platter of shredded lettuce and place egg rolls thereon. Cut each roll into 3 pieces, or serve each person one whole roll and let him cut his own. This recipe yields 8 egg rolls approximately. Serve with soy and mustard paste.

SOUPS

•●•

Soup Base—(Chinese)

Boil 8 cups water. Add 1 whole chicken carcass (plus other chicken bones you may have stashed away in the freezer), giblets, a good handful of pork bones (or ½-lb. piece of pork or 1 lb. of pork neck), a stalk of celery, a ½-inch slice of ginger and salt. A small piece of *chung choi* (salted turnip) that has been washed well could be added during the simmering process. This is optional but does give a very nice flavor. *Chung choi* is usually sold in plastic bags and quite pungent; be prepared for strong odors and repack when you get home. The turnips may dry out but they never spoil—the salt preserves them forever and ever.

Simmer, covered, for 1 hour and strain. Remove excess fat. If flavor is weak you could add a chicken-base stock extender or a bouillon cube. Add 1 tsp. MSG and more salt, if desired. A pinch of sugar helps flavor, too. Add ½ cup fresh mushrooms, sliced thin, ½ cup Oriental vegetables such as bamboo shoots, sliced, or water chestnuts, sliced. Cook just long enough to bring the vegetables to a very crisp tender stage. Serve.

Other variations with this soup base:

Add a handful of peas.

Some bits of thin seaweed (*nori* or *wakame*) can be added for a different flavor. *Wakame* should be soaked 10 minutes in water. Drain and rinse to remove sediment.

For egg drop soup (sometimes called "Flower Soup") add 2 eggs, slightly beaten, very slowly to the simmering soup. Drip it from a distance so the egg will hit the bubbling soup surface. Stir while doing so. It helps to separate the egg into shreds.

Dehydrated chicken noodle soups make fine emergency soup bases for *won ton*. Make it Oriental by adding some chopped green onions and Chinese parsley. A dish of soy with a few drops of sesame oil for a dipping sauce with the soup is usually served.

For *won ton* soup, pour hot soup base over boiled *won tons* (already placed in individual bowls). Garnish with a spinach leaf and slivered green onions. As you remove the *won ton* ready to eat, add soy with chopsticks to the spoon holding the *won ton*.

You could serve boiled noodles in a bowl and pour over hot soup with garnishes. Other vegetables that could be used for variety: *Nappa* cabbage, *bok choy*, dried and soaked Oriental mushrooms or edible-pod peas. Eliminate some of the original soup vegetables. Serve in a large soup tureen. Have some soy sauce with a few drops of sesame oil, chopped green onions and Chinese parsley for condiments.

Greens Soup (Chinese)

6 cups soup stock or commercial chicken broth
1 cup lean pork meat, sliced thin
several slices ¼-inch thick fresh ginger

about 1 pound or 3 cups greens such as *nappa* cabbage, *bok choy* or mustard, sliced in 1-inch lengths

Bring stock to boil. Add ginger. Put in pork and simmer for about 10 minutes. Add greens. Cook for about 2 more minutes. Be sure to keep the greens nice and crisp. Season with salt and MSG. A few drops of sesame oil and soy can be added, but, just a little bit.

Winter Melon Soup (Chinese)

6 cups soup stock (pork or chicken) or substitute commercial chicken broth
1 lb. winter melon, peeled and sliced into neat chunks
1 cup cooked pork or chicken slices (you can mix both, if you like)
4 dried Oriental mushrooms,

soaked, drained and sliced thin
½ cup bamboo shoots, sliced, or substitute sliced water chestnuts
dash of MSG
2 tsp. soy
dash of grated ginger
dash of sugar
salt to taste

Bring stock to boil and add melon, mushrooms and bamboo. Cook about 20 minutes. Add seasonings. Simmer a few minutes.

Add the cooked meat. Heat through. Adjust seasonings. Garnish with chopped green onions. A few drops of sesame oil will enhance the flavor.

A good substitute for the winter melon could be *chayote*—a Mexican vegetable available in supermarkets. Or try cucumbers, sliced, with the seeds removed. Fuzzy or hairy squash (*mo gwa*), peeled and cut into small pieces is good too.

Fish Soup (Japanese)

Simmer a fresh fish head (like sea bass) for 15 minutes with about 4 cups of water. Add ginger slice, salt and dash of MSG. Strain and serve with a few pieces of cubed bean cake (*tofu*), and slices of green onions. Perhaps a thin sliver of lemon peel could be added. Should be very clear and most delicate in flavor. A drop or two of soy is permissible but too much will destroy the nice subtle quality of a good Japanese soup.

Cloudy Mist Soup (Japanese)

Make about 5 cups of Japanese broth (*dashi*) using the instant fish and seaweed type base. Bring to simmering and add ⅓ to ½ cup white soy bean paste (*shiro miso*) blending carefully little by little. Bring it near boiling and lower heat to keep simmering. Add small cubes of soy bean cake (*tofu*) and garnish with a few sprinkles of chopped green onions. A piece of seaweed (*wakame*), soaked for 10 minutes in water and rinsed, could be added to the soup. Cut the *wakame* in short lengths before cooking. Simmer for 1 minute and serve.

Tranquil Beauty Soup (Japanese)

This is the basic soup for Japanese cookery and can be made quite simply in our modern kitchens. Rather a champagne-color with very delicate flavorings, the clear soup can be made with instant fish and seaweed broth prepared from a product that looks like tea bags. Do not over cook in the preparation of this soup base (*dashi*) since bitterness develops.

Strain and use your creative imagination to decorate with attractive garnishes. Use petite cubes of white soy bean cake and a leaf of spinach with, perhaps a thin slice of lemon peel. Or, try a slice of steamed fish cake (*kamaboko*) with its rim of red over a half-circle of off-white color, a sprig of edible chrysanthemum leaf and a few very slender shreds of orange carrot. Even a garnish of a flower-shaped carrot will do nicely with a thin slice of lime for a bit of whimsical, gossamer appearance.

This soup base can be used with boiled noodles to make a most satisfying noodle soup, adding roast pork slices, a half of a boiled egg and a dash of chopped green onions. In the preparation of Japanese-style soup, one can always substitute chicken broth for convenience and for a less fishy taste—it may suit you better.

GARNISHES

The talented Orientals excel as garnish designers. You can use these types of garnishes for decorations on Western-style salads—macaroni and potato, Jello salads—on meat dishes and so forth. The Orientals, especially the Japanese, do not just use a bunch of parsley and call it finished. They might use parsley but they make it very creative and most artistic, like a picture. One feasts with his eyes as well as his mouth in Japanese cuisine. Occasionally, the artistic flare is more satisfying than the taste. The outward appearance—the intensity of the eye appeal of the foods served to us—often makes it appetizing or not. The garnish is an extra fillip, accenting a perfect culinary effort.

One of the simplest methods of making garnishes with vegetables is to use a set of Japanese stainless steel cutters, similar to cookie cutters. You can press down on your firm and fresh vegetables, i.e., carrots, turnips, *daikon* (radish), yam and whatever you wish to use to form artistic flower shapes. The cutters come in all sizes. The Japanese cutters which are about 2 inches high and about 1 inch in diameter can be used for garnishes as well as miniature canapes or cookies. The ½-inch or ¾-inch diameter by 1 inch ones work well for daintier garnishes. You can even cut petite cookies with these Japanese decorative cutters.

Chinese parsley (fresh coriander) as well as Chinese pepper or Japanese *sansho* (fresh) leaves make beautiful green touches to any dish. *Ti* leaves from Hawaii or aspidistra leaves from our gardens can be used as a dark green garnish. Often, the aspidistra leaf is cut into a zig-zag pointed design. These design-cut leaves could be laid flat or be supported between foods, such as *sushi,* much like a fence decor.

ONION SPRAY FLOWERS OR BRUSHES (CHINESE)

Remove roots from green onions—cut 5 or 6 lengths, about 2 inches long, from the white root section of as many green onion stalks. At each end, make four slashes one-third of the way down. Place in ice water and the slashed ends will flare open into flowers with curls. Often these onion sprays are used as garnishes on the platters of Chinese entrees. At the same time, they can serve as miniature edible brushes for putting sauces, such as *hoisin,* on your bun along with Peking duck slices.

PLUM BLOSSOM EGGS (JAPANESE)

Hard cook eggs 7 to 10 minutes. Stir a few seconds when water starts to boil in order to center the yolk. Shell while still warm and dip in water containing red food coloring until they are a pleasing reddish-pink color. Do not get eggs too dark. Remove from food dye and place while still warm into the form and chill.

To make the form: Cut a 1-inch slice of raw potato and insert 5 chopsticks in a circle using the potato as a stand. The circle should be slightly under the circumference of the egg so when the eggs are inserted the whites will slightly bulge out between the sticks.

After placing 2 or 3 eggs in the form, secure the stick ends with a rubber band. Be sure eggs are cold and set before removing from mold. To serve, remove eggs and slice cross-wise and you will have pretty plum blossoms.

With 4 sticks in your potato stand you could form a shamrock with green colored eggs for St. Patrick's Day. With some ingenuity, like using a heart shaped cookie cutter you can jam a warm egg in the cutter, and the result could be a heart for Valentine's Day. There are limitless ways to make these beautiful garnishes and they can be prepared ahead and refrigerated. Here again is beauty that a Japanese person would see in an egg.

VEGETABLE FLOWERS

Carrots, turnips and *daikon* radish make attractive garnish flowers. Cut grooves the full length of the outside of the peeled vegetable. Make thin slices for a decorative flower. Trim with lemon peel shreds for stamens or take the same grooved vegetable and cut a cone at one end. Shave with a very sharp knife in a circular way the full circle shape of the vegetable making a sort of cup flower. Put in lemon peel stamens. Thin, plain edged turnip slices can be rolled and held in place with picks to form calla lilies! With practice, one could invent more combinations.

TOMATO ROSES

Select even shaped tomatoes with good color. Cover with boiling water; let stand 1 minute. Remove, and let cool. With a paring knife, starting from the bottom of tomato, remove skin in one spiral by cutting circular fashion around the tomato. Wind the skin loosely around a chopstick, folding back edges of skin as you wind, to give petal effect. Carefully remove the wooden stick. Refrigerate the rose until ready to use.

Another method for the roses: select your good ripe tomatoes and simply peel the skin in one continuous paring. Shape the peel into a rose by cupping in your hand. Spread the petals to make it look like a rose. The peeled tomato can be used for salads.

LOTUS LACE FLOWERS

Fresh lotus root, peeled and thinly sliced, makes a beautiful garnish just as is, since there are many odd shaped holes in the lotus root itself to give it a very delicate lacy effect.

VEGETABLES, SALADS, NOODLES
●●■●●

HOW TO USE SEAWEED

Seaweed is actually a plant of the sea and no different from any other type of cultivated plant that we grow on land. But somehow we Americans have preconceived ideas about seaweed, perhaps because we do not commonly use it in our food pattern.

In America, there is presently serious thought of sea farming if we are to survive and have enough food to feed the hungry. Seaweed and kelp are healthful foods full of minerals and vitamins. One of the principal elements derived from seaweed is iodine. This prevents goiter. You rarely see anyone with goiter problems in the Orient.

When I use *wakame* (lobe leaf seaweed) in class, some people have commented that it looks just like the "icky" stuff we drag around the sandy beaches. True! But, the fantastic marvel is that it is one of the most highly nutritious foods of the world. Certain varieties are a true delicacy.

"Ocean" Salad (Japanese)

1 can crabmeat, shrimp, abalone (small size can) or equivalent amount of fresh seafood — about 1 cup — even cooked octopus, sliced, is good

6 strips of Japanese dried seaweed (*wakame*) about 7 to 8 inches long to equal about 1 cup when soaked
1 rib of celery or half of a cucumber
omelet made with 1 or 2 eggs

Shred crabmeat (or leave small local shrimps whole or julienne strip abalone). Julienne strip the celery or the cucumber. Soak *wakame* in cold water to cover until soft, about 10 minutes. Drain. Rinse to remove sand sediment. Cut into ½-inch lengths. (Some persons remove all the heavy parts of the *wakame,* however, I

find it adds to the chewiness that is desirable and use all of it.)
Make a thin omelet with 1 or 2 eggs diluting slightly beaten egg
with a bit of water or stock. Fry omelet in slightly oiled frying
pan at medium temperature. Let cool and cut into short julienne
strips. Mix seafood, *wakame,* vegetable and egg strips in bowl.

In another bowl make the following dressing:

6 Tbsp. rice wine vinegar	½ tsp. soy
2 Tbsp. or more sugar	1 tsp. MSG or less
1 Tbsp. water	½ to 1 tsp. ginger juice or
½ tsp. salt	grated ginger

Toss salad just before serving. This is also a very low calorie
dressing for any green salad you decide to use.

Note: Do not oversoak *wakame*. It will soften and get mushy.
You want the chewy quality to remain in the *wakame*. This is a
developed taste but much more pleasant than you might imagine!

VARIETIES OF SEAWEED

Laver seaweed (*nori*) comes in thin sheets rather purplish-
black. There are all kinds of qualities from fair to excellent. The
inexpensive types are usually used for soups and the most expensive quality is reserved for Japanese rice rolls (*nori-maki*).
One should toast on one side over a heat source for the bringing
out of the best flavors.

Tangle seaweed is *konbu* and used for soup flavoring as well
as cooked and eaten with meat and vegetables. It has a certain
soft, chewy texture. Again, it is not something you would jump
up and down with joy the first time you sample it. But, on the
other hand, it has an exquisite, unexplainable taste quality that
makes the Japanese, especially, like it.

The agar seaweed (*kanten*) in its commercial form looks like
transparent glass shreds. When dissolved in hot water, it sets when
cooled very similarly to our unflavored gelatin; with the one difference that it will get firm at room temperature. There is also
a much firmer quality to agar-agar. None of the quiver we have
come to associate with Jello. Agar-agar is the gelatinous product
used for bacterial cultures in research labs.

Cellophane Shreds With Ham (Chinese)

This looks like a shredded plastic bag salad!

4 sticks Japanese *kanten* (agar-agar), white, or use equivalent Chinese agar-agar threads (about 1 oz.)
4 slices ham
1 Tbsp. soy
1 tsp. sesame oil
1 Tbsp. toasted sesame seeds
½ tsp. salt
½ tsp. sugar
dash MSG
1 green onion, chopped or shredded

Soak agar-agar in *cold* water for 5 minutes or even a bit longer. Drain. Wash well to clean the sediment that sometimes is lodged in the sticks. Squeeze dry. Cut into tiny shreds. Cut ham into match stick strips. Mix soy, oil, salt, sugar, MSG and onions. Add to the agar-agar and mix. Garnish with the ham and the sesame seeds. Serve cold. Be careful not to use hot water with the agar-agar or it will melt.

Variations: Use other nuts and any leftover cold meat.

NOODLES

Making loud slurping noises in eating noodles is considered fine etiquette in both Japan and China. I think they feel noodles taste better this way. The Orientals do not even notice the noises while they suck in like a vacuum cleaner—so contrary to our American way of thinking. Here is another point of interest. I observe that many Orientals remove their eye glasses when they eat noodles. The steam just fogs them up, so, one might just as well be practical! How difficult it is to bring up a family and tell them, "You can make noise with Oriental noodles but when you have American-style noodle soup do not lift your bowl—do not slurp—do not this or that!" No wonder that in this American culture of ours, which is truly a conglomeration of international cultures, there are contradictions that require a psychologist to help untangle! I feel there is truth in the saying that in the Orient everything is upside down from America.

Saimin, Instant Ramen and Udon

Saimin is a Hawaiian version of Oriental soup with noodles. It is now available in many instant versions. The instant *ramen* is practically a duplicate of *saimin*.

In the past decade, instant noodles have been flooding the market. The seasonings and flavorings are basically Japanese although many have Chinese flavors. These instant precooked noodles require only a short 2 to 3 minutes of cooking time. There is a multitude of varieties and if you add a few fresh chopped green onions and a slice of hard cooked egg they can achieve a "like-fresh" flavor. Billions of packets are selling annually. For a quick lunch, snack or for plain convenience they are great! Rather austere food for gourmets, however. Many of the other instant-type foods being imported from the Orient are not very satisfactory and shortly after introduction many of them fade away—poor imitations of the real products.

Japanese Udon

Udon is a thick noodle made from either wheat or corn flour; probably the closest American-style noodle it can be compared with is our thick spaghetti.

Take 1 lb. Japanese *udon* (dry noodles—usually sold in bundles wrapped in thin plastic wrap or in boxes—not the precooked instant types). Use a large pot and fill three-quarters full with water. Bring to boil and place *udon* in carefully, in full lengths. Do not add all at once but give a stir between additions with long chopsticks. They will not stick to the bottom of pan if you do this. Continue boiling until noodles become rather rounded at the edges instead of squarish. Add a cup of cold water to the boiling pot. Do this about three times. Boil a total of 12-15 minutes.

Test one noodle by dropping in cold water to cool. Chew and see if it is tender. Do not overcook. Keep it *al dente*. Another very unorthodox test I used to see actually done, and one that really works, is to take one hot noodle from the pot and throw it with vigor against the wall. If it sticks to the wall, it's just right. Wow! How about a wall full of stuck noodles? An abstract and three dimensional design at that! Remove cooked noodles from stove, place noodles in colander and wash thoroughly with cold water using hands to run through the noodles. Drain. Should not be sticky. Serve hot or cold. If serving hot, pass the noodles through some boiling water just before placing in *donburi* bowls (large, deep ceramic bowl). This will reheat the noodles. Serve with variously flavored broths such as commercial chicken soup, Japanese seaweed and fish soup base made from assorted instant soup mixes or whatever soup you desire. Serve miscellaneous condiments such as *daikon-oroshi* (finely grated Japanese radish), grated ginger, finely chopped green onions and toasted seaweed (*nori*), crumbled. Attractive garnishes could be one poached egg or hard cooked egg slices, neat slices of chicken or pork plus a few slices of red colored fish cake (*kamaboko*), a few pieces of green spinach and a few strands of yellow egg strips. The Chinese soup base of pork and chicken flavor also makes a good soup for these noodles. Do not, however, reverse this and use Japanese soup base for Chinese-style soups or foods. The taste is not like the Chinese flavors.

Use soy to personal tastes on the noodles. To serve cold, as is often done in the hot summer months, place several ice cubes in each bowl along with the noodles. Garnish with shrimp that has been cooked previously for about three minutes in boiling water, perhaps a seasoned dried Japanese mushroom (*shiitake*) which, too, has been properly flavored with some soy and a bit of sugar, and to complete the vision you could add a small leaf of green spinach. You serve this with a dipping sauce made with Japanese soup base and with additions of *mirin* (sweet rice wine), soy, salt and MSG. A thinner noodle called *hiyamugi* is usually used for this dish, but one could experiment with the *udon.*

Chow Mein (Chinese)

Fresh egg noodles make the tastiest *chow mein.* I am not referring to the Americanized *chow mein* version of deep-fried crispy noodles but to the Cantonese pan-fried style. Fresh noodles can be made with any noodle recipe since they are all practically the same base. However, there is so much work involved, most of us prefer to buy the packaged fresh noodles in the delicatessen departments of the markets. If you cannot find the Chinese egg noodles fresh, a good substitute is Italian fresh *taglarini* (egg noodles).

Fresh egg noodles freeze very well so buy extra from the store when you see them. Wrap well in foil or put in plastic bags for good storage. It prevents freezer burn or drying out.

If you should want to make the American version of crispy noodles, just drop the fresh egg noodles into deep-fat. They will cook very quickly and get nice and brown. Drain and make the regular *chow mein* sauce to pour over all.

Pork Chow Mein (Chinese Cantonese Style)

1 or 1½ lbs. fresh noodles, pan-fried
1½ lbs. pork, sliced ⅛-inch-by-1½-inch strips (could be loin, butt, chops, leg)
1 clove garlic, minced
½ tsp. grated ginger
1 medium onion, cut in rings then in half
3 or 4 ribs celery, cut into very thin strips (the thick ribs of the outer part of a celery stalk could be slashed into layers and then placed on top of each other to be sliced into thin strips diagonally)
1 small can bamboo shoots, cut into thin strips or 1 small can water chestnuts, sliced in very thin strips

1 cup fresh edible-pod peas, cut in thin strips or use half a package of thawed frozen regular peas (we can't help these regular peas being round when everything else in this recipe conforms to strips —besides, most persons would not even know the uniform-size idea of Chinese cooking)
½ lb. fresh bean sprouts, washed and drained
1 cup fresh mushrooms, sliced thin or 3 large Japanese dried mushrooms, soaked in water, squeezed dry and cut into thin strips
salt to taste (about 1 tsp.)

GRAVY:

2 Tbsp. soy
1½ Tbsp. cornstarch
1 tsp. MSG
1 Tbsp. sherry wine

1 tsp. sugar
1 tsp. sesame oil
1 cup water or stock

GARNISH AND CONDIMENTS:

2 or 3 stalks of green onions, shredded thin
Chinese parsley leaves (optional)
roast pork, cut into thin strips (optional, but nice!)

oil, salt and pepper
cider vinegar or lemon wedges (optional)
mustard paste (optional)
egg omelet strips (optional)

Brown pork with salt, garlic and ginger in a hot oiled frying pan. Add gravy ingredients and thicken. (This should not take too long.) Remove from pan. Sauté celery, onion and bamboo shoots (or water chestnuts) in 1 Tbsp. oil for one minute over high heat; salt and add to pork. Sauté peas, bean sprouts and mushrooms with 1 Tbsp. oil; salt. Add the pork and gravy with all of the vegetable mixture to the peas, etc. mixture in pan. Heat for half a minute, toss-frying together lightly with chopsticks and spread over the prepared noodles. If you like more gravy you could add more water while you are heating up the mixture. You could use a lesser quantity of noodles (about 1 lb. or less) and this will keep the pork mixture more juicy. But I find some people want a lot of extra noodles; in fact, there are those that like just noodles. Arrange fried noodles on platter and pour pork and vegetable mixture over all. Or toss-fry noodles with the pork and vegetables 1 minute in the pan. This blends the flavor nicely together. Garnish with chopped green onions, egg strips, parsley or whatever you like. Serve with soy, vinegar and mustard in little dishes.

Good substitutes for the pork are raw chicken, remains of a chicken, turkey or pork roast. This is a good way to use leftover turkey instead of the usual *a la king* methods. In fact, your family will never recognize the turkey flavor!

Egg Garnish for Chow Mein

To 2 eggs, add dash of salt, dash MSG and drop of sherry. Blend together. Pour small amount of the mixture into a hot, very lightly oiled skillet, spread evenly in pan. Cook egg over low heat until set and dry. Use cover, if necessary. Electric skillet works very nicely. Repeat as many times as needed to use up egg mixture. Place these thin crepes on top of each other. They freeze well so make more, if desired. Slice in thin strips of desired size —long or short, but thin in width.

Pan-Fried Noodles (Cantonese Style)

Boil 2 quarts of water and 1 Tbsp. of oil in a large pot, one that will hold a deep-fry basket or sieve. You can use a regular deep-fry pan and basket set. Separate the fresh egg noodles and loosen the whole 1 lb. bagful on a paper towel or wherever it is convenient. They have a tendency to stick together. Drop about ½ lb. of noodles at a time into the basket, stirring noodles to prevent melding together. Scald for 20 seconds. Stir vigorously at the same time.

Lift basket and drain off excess water. Run noodles under warm water or have a large pot of water near the stove so you can wash off the excess starch. Have ready a heavy frying pan over high heat with a thin layer of oil—about 2 Tbsp. Brown on one side and then the other, adding more oil when necessary, dripping from edges into the pan. Cover your work area with newspapers to catch the spatters. The *wok* works wonders for making this dish—especially for frying the noodles. The wet noodles will be dripping with water when you put them in the oiled pan so be careful. They spatter all over the place.

Watch carefully since this does burn if there is not enough oil. You want a golden brown color, crisp on the outside and soft inside, for the noodle pancakes. Drain on paper towels and keep warm while you prepare the pork and vegetable mixture. If you should decide to make a large quantity of noodles, change the water in the pot occasionally since the boiling water will become thick and starchy. Cut fried noodles with a knife into serving portions to make serving easier, or just use your fingers to tear the pancakes apart. This is now ready for the sauce.

One lb. fresh noodles with *chow mein* sauce will serve 3 or 4 persons. This is something like spaghetti—people consume a lot! This *chow mein* sauce alone makes a type of *chow yuk* or *chop suey* (which is really not a Chinese dish—it was invented in America) dish, if served without the noodles and with steaming hot rice.

The noodles could be fried in advance and warmed up just before use. However, do not keep in the warm oven too long. They will dry out and get terribly hard.

CHOW YUK (CHINESE)

The basis of *chow yuk* dishes is mixed vegetables with meat. *Chop suey* (truly not Chinese in origin but probably devised in America by the early Chinese workers) is of this same family. This is a most versatile recipe. Use whatever vegetables you have on hand and whatever meat is available. Do not be afraid to combine suitable vegetables with whatever meat you have. The Chinese even combine pork with shrimp, pork with chicken, and so on. This type of recipe helps balance dishes that might be mainly all protein such as fish, meat, poultry. This is a good family-type dish and the vegetables taste so much better this way, even children will gobble up what they might ignore if the ingredients had been prepared simply as boiled vegetables.

Chow Yuk With Chinese Cabbage (Nappa) or Whatever Your Refrigerator Yields

¾ to 1 lb. fresh raw pork, sliced thin
1 clove garlic, minced
½ tsp. ginger, grated
1 medium onion, sliced thin
2 lbs. vegetables, such as Chinese cabbage (*nappa*), celery, peppers, tomatoes, onions, bean sprouts, asparagus, carrots, broccoli, cabbage, mustard greens, bamboo shoots, string beans, water chestnuts, brussels sprouts and so on, cut uniformly to desired size and shape

GRAVY:

2 tsp. soy
2 Tbsp. sherry
1 tsp. salt or more
¼ cup soup stock, or water (you may wish to add more)
1 Tbsp. cornstarch (more, if thick sauce desired)
1 tsp. MSG
½ tsp. sugar
dash of pepper

Mix gravy ingredients and have ready for use. Put 1 Tbsp. oil in a hot skillet. Place over highest heat until smoking. Add pork, garlic and ginger. Toss-fry until the meat is cooked. Add the gravy ingredients. Heat. Add onion and vegetables that you have decided to use. Stir and toss-fry all the time. Cover, if necessary, to quicken the cooking process. This depends upon the vegetables that are used, such as string beans, carrots, and other firmer vegetables. You may slice or chunk the vegetables as you desire. Keep size uniform. Do not overcook. Keep crisp! It takes just minutes to accomplish this desired crisp-tender texture, so watch carefully.

I often go to the refrigerator with a tray and get all the potential vegetables that I want to use and start cutting. When I have enough I return what I didn't need. This is a marvelous way to use up bits of assorted vegetable accumulations—as well as a good way to end up with vegetables still leftover because you had too much to use up in the first place! Keep trying!

ORIENTAL EGGPLANT

These thin, long tender eggplants are claimed by many countries as "their" vegetable. Japan considers it theirs, too. A very delicate vegetable, more so than the large round ones most of us are used to seeing in the markets. They are becoming more common and most likely you will find them in your larger city markets. There is one way you can have them despite distance from a source of supply. Grow your own! They are no more difficult than the big eggplants. They produce abundantly.

Eggplants (Japanese)

Pan-fry in a bit of vegetable oil whole unpeeled Japanese eggplants very quickly, turning often, about 5 minutes. They will become soft. Serve with soy sauce and MSG. Good with *teriyaki* and bowls of hot, steaming rice.

How to Prepare Eggplant Slices

Not Oriental, but different. Slice into ½-inch slices. Place on broiler rack. Brush ever so lightly with mayonnaise (use a pastry brush). Broil for 5 minutes until browned. Turn over. You can again brush on more mayonnaise, but, usually I do not. Broil until brown. Serve with soy. Good while broiling chops, steaks, and so on.

Another Even Simpler Method

Place whole unpeeled eggplant (large American type), washed, into oven when preparing roast or ham. Put this eggplant directly on rack of oven. No need to soil a baking pan. Bake at 350°F. for about 45 minutes until soft when touched by hands. Cut or break open in half. Add seasonings, either with butter, salt and pepper or Oriental style with soy and MSG.

Eggplant With Sake (Japanese)

1 medium eggplant	½ tsp. MSG
1 Tbsp. oil	2 Tbsp. *sake* (Japanese rice
2 Tbsp. soy	wine) or sherry or use up
2 Tbsp. sugar	to ¼ cup

Wash eggplant and cut into ¾-inch cubes. Heat oil, add eggplant and sauté. Add soy, sugar, MSG and *sake* or sherry. Cover and cook until done and thickened a bit, about 5 minutes.

Broiled Green Peppers (Japanese)

Quarter bell peppers, remove stems and seeds. Lightly brush with oil and broil over charcoal or in oiled skillet. Turn once. Do not overcook; 4 to 6 minutes should be ample time. Should be semi-crisp. Serve with soy.

Fried Asparagus (Chinese)

2 to 3 lbs. asparagus	½ tsp. salt
1 Tbsp. oil	½ tsp. MSG
ginger slice and garlic, crushed (spear on toothpick for easy recovery later)	dash of sugar and pepper, if desired

Break off woody ends of asparagus. Wash carefully since

there is often sand imbedded in stalks. Cut diagonally into ½-inch slices. Heat oil in hot frying pan. Add garlic and ginger and sauté for ½ minute. Add asparagus and sprinkle with salt, MSG and sugar. Stir toss-fry with spatula over high heat for 2 to 3 minutes. Test a piece. Should be crunchy. Serve soy with dish. Remove ginger and garlic before serving. Use any vegetables you wish this way.

Brussels Sprouts (Chinese)

This method of vegetable preparation is basic and is a family favorite. It is typically Chinese-style—not the brussels sprouts—but the crunchy, good texture and delectable flavor. Goes with Oriental foods or with steaks, hamburgers or just by itself.

Clean and slice firm brussels sprouts in ⅛-inch slices from the top toward the root section. Wash and drain. Sear a piece of ginger and a crushed piece of garlic in a hot oiled pan. Add sliced brussels sprouts. Toss-fry 3 minutes, adding salt, pepper and dashes of MSG and sugar. If there is a tendency for the vegetables to be too dry, add a few tablespoons of hot water so that everything will steam a bit while it is being toss-fried. Substitute cauliflower or regular cannon ball cabbage. Remove ginger and garlic before serving. Good just as is or serve with soy.

DRIED MUSHROOMS (CHINESE OR JAPANESE)

These imported mushrooms are seemingly most expensive, especially the large Japanese *shiitake,* but they stretch a long way. A few used in this recipe and in that give you a flavor you cannot achieve with fresh fungus. There are several different varieties on the market. Some are rather dark brownish-black and large, while others are smaller and shaped more like a flower-cap.

I do warn that one should not go to extremes with Oriental ingredients. Too much of the overwhelming, powerful, earthy flavor of dried mushrooms would spoil many a dish, where a few would have made it a gourmet's delight—so subtle, exquisite and fit for the most particular critic. Just because you like the intense mushroom flavor, do not go overboard and use it in all your cooking. Soon your American, European, Far East concoctions will all begin to have that familiar Oriental touch. Certainly this is the worst thing that could happen. You want individual flavors representative of every school of cooking, otherwise, everything will become monotonous and uninteresting. The idea in learning the many international dishes is to retain the identity of each. Surely if you like soy, for instance, poured on top of beef steak—fine! It's delicious and I like it, too. But don't overuse it. Use restraint. The same applies to the mushrooms.

How to Prepare Dried Mushrooms for Use

The ideal is to soak dried mushrooms for 20 minutes in warm water. (Do not oversoak. The rich flavor you paid for will be diluted.) Remove heavy stems. This water can be used for liquid in recipes if you are careful not to get the sediment that may have settled at the bottom. Squeeze water out and use according to recipe instructions. A bit of sugar will speed the softening of the dried product when soaking in water. In a dire emergency, I have even taken a few dried mushrooms and gone to the hot water tap and performed a sort of massaging action. The fungi have plumped up enough for me to cut them up for use! But this is the unforgivable method. Try not to get into this sort of predicament. Read your recipe well in advance of preparation.

The Oriental dried mushrooms have a different flavor from the European varieties but try this "quickie." Soak and squeeze dry as many dried mushrooms as you desire. Then, fry them in butter seasoned with salt and MSG. They are tasty this way, but expensive to prepare, especially these days when fresh mushrooms are retailing at very low prices.

GARLIC

Indispensable in Chinese cookery. When clove of garlic is mentioned in recipe use about the size of the tip of your "pinky" or baby finger. Place unpeeled clove of garlic on cutting board and smash with gentle pressure using side of cleaver blade or end of knife handle. Outer skin will slip right off. Your garlic will be crushed and hardly a trace of garlic odor is under your fingernails. To deodorize this pungency from hands use a bit of lemon juice.

GINGER

I use fresh ginger root only and NEVER substitute powdered ginger from the spice shelves. Depending upon the many varieties hitting the markets, some are more grey while others are more yellow. They can be used interchangeably. If I do not have any on hand, I leave it out of the recipe.

The stores are all beginning to sell the fresh gnarled roots. If you cannot get it fresh often, here are ways to keep it and still have the fresh flavor retained over months. Buy it when you see it, especially if it is nice and firm and not shriveled up.

You will find that cooking brings out the full flavor of the fresh ginger root. It is also used uncooked and grated as a condiment. Other forms of ginger such as ground, crystallized and preserved are better used in sweetened dishes. It is known as a deodorizer for cooking fish. I like to think its main job is adding flavor—a very pleasant delicate one.

Keep it unwrapped on the refrigerator shelf. It develops a dehydrated outside skin and retains its fresh quality for grating, etc. Peel it each time or if no one's looking (or, if you are a casual cook) grate it peel and all. Who will know?

You can also freeze it whole. Grate it while it is hard and frozen. Use it in a larger quantity, however, since the flavor is lost somewhat in freezing. Another method is to grate or slice a whole ginger root into a small half-pint jar filled partially with sherry. This will give you sherry plus ginger and most recipes use ginger and sherry. If not, add sherry anyway, it will benefit rather than spoil your entree.

Some persons I know keep the root buried in wet sand and dig it up each time they need it. I do not find this too practical. I'd have to take it out of the pot everyday!

Usually, Chinese recipes call for slices of ginger. If you use it thus, invariably one of your dear family will bite into a piece and never again will they want to venture into the exotic tastes of the Oriental. So, I have been using only grated style, using one of those handy Japanese graters. The flavors can get "married" beautifully, without resulting in ginger-haters.

BEAN THREADS (SAI FUN, LONG RICE, CELLOPHANE NOODLES) (CHINESE)

Bean threads are made from the starch of mung beans. It is tough to break the wiry strands. The way I have devised to attack what looks like a tangle of transparent wires is to place the whole batch in a large, heavy grocery bag. Take your kitchen shears and cut into strands the width of the bundle. At least, if it is all in one bag you can work with it easier. Otherwise, it will end up with bits of crisp, crackly pieces all over the floors. If you know how slippery a few strands can be, you will also use my method, and save some near misses slipping on the floor. A most dangerous situation.

Soak in hot water 20 minutes for use. This softens the bean threads so that they become pliable. Cut in 2-inch pieces or whatever your recipe requires. It has no flavor of its own, but acquires taste of the cooking juices. *Sai fun* has a chewy, gelatinous texture that most persons like.

In most recipes, you can substitute vermicelli for bean threads. Add just before ready to serve—about 5 minutes before, just long enough to heat through and flavor. Many Chinese recipes use bean thread mixed stir-fry fashion with meat or shell fish and vegetables. Japanese also use bean thread for salads and as a substitute for *shiratoki* (yam noodles) in *sukiyaki*. It is less expensive and most Occidentals seem to prefer it over the *shirataki*.

Bean Threads With Ham (Japanese)

½ lb. boiled ham, cut julienne strips	a handful of *sai fun* (bean thread) soaked in hot water for 15 minutes to equal 1½ cup soaked bean thread
2 cucumbers, peeled and cut julienne strips	
1 tsp. grated ginger	

SAUCE:

1 Tbsp. mustard (dry)	3 Tbsp. rice wine vinegar
3 tsp. sugar	3 tsp. soy
1 tsp. salt	dash of MSG

Peel cucumbers. Cut into half lengthwise removing seeds, if too large. Cut into julienne strips. Add salt and mix. Slice ham into strips. Put bean thread in boiling water and turn off heat. Let stand for 10 to 15 minutes. When transparent, drain in colander, then cut into 1-inch lengths. Cool. Mix the remaining ingredients 5 minutes before serving. Add cucumber, ham and the bean threads and mix. Clams, shrimps, crab or sliced steamed fishcake *(kamaboko)* could be used. Adjust seasonings.

ASSORTED SALADS (JAPANESE)

Truthfully, the Japanese and the Chinese do not have so-called salads as we know them. The following Japanese style dishes are basically vinegared varieties *(sunomono)* that could nicely fall into the category of salad. Combined with any of our Occidental meals they would be nice, too.

Chrysanthemum-Shaped Turnips (Japanese)

The average modern American would say "No" if asked about his liking for turnips. Surprisingly, with this method of preparation many have become turnip addicts. You will no doubt become converted too.

4 or 5 good-shaped turnips	grows for you
1 fresh lemon for its unblemished peel	¾ tsp. salt
	dash MSG
chrysanthemum leaves or whatever your garden	1½ Tbsp. sugar
	6 Tbsp. rice wine vinegar

Cut large turnips in half. Make very thin cross-wise slices from the top, three-fourths of the way to the bottom of the turnip. It's a good idea to put chopsticks on each side of the turnip as you slice so that the knife will not cut through. Slice criss-cross the opposite way (perpendicularly to the first cut). Sprinkle with

¾ tsp. salt and allow to stand until soft. After about 15 minutes, squeeze tightly to remove all the excess liquids.

Sprinkle 2 Tbsp. vinegar over the turnips and stir. Squeeze the vinegar out of the turnips. Discard juices.

Mix 4 Tbsp. vinegar, 1½ Tbsp. sugar and a dash of MSG and add to turnips. Let this stand for several hours, stirring occasionally for the flavors to blend. Wash the leaves and spread them on a colorful platter. Arrange the flower-shaped turnips and in the center of each "chrysanthemum" add a small piece of lemon rind. The "petals" will be very limp so you can open them up to make them appear more like real flowers.

I like to make a few large turnips and then with the remaining turnips make multitudes of small cubes. Make by reversing the large turnips after making the criss-cross cuts and partially cutting down on the turnips in small cube size. Break off the segments before marinating.

This way, I can have the elegance of several large "flowers" and everyone can consume the cubes first. Eventually the large ones can be eaten too. Variations: A few drops of red food coloring can be added during marinating to make lovely pink blooms. Remember for the Japanese, visual beauty in food presentation is most important.

A simplified cutting method for the turnips is to make sheer slices only and follow the directions—less time consuming, especially for family servings and just as tasty!

Watercress and Bean Sprout Salad

Watercress—be sure to soak covered in cold water with salt. This will make any of the "creatures" in the tubular stems wiggle out. Rinse well in several waters. Drain in colander.

1 large bunch of watercress, cut in 1-inch lengths	2 or 3 Tbsp. toasted sesame seeds, white or black
½ lb. fresh bean sprouts	3 Tbsp. rice wine vinegar
½ tsp. salt	3 Tbsp. sugar
1 tsp. finely chopped fresh ginger	dash of MSG

Parboil bean sprouts for 1 minute in boiling water. Pass cold water through the hot bean sprouts to stop the cooking process. Drain. Put bean sprouts in a bowl. Add watercress and salt. Toss carefully. Combine remaining ingredients and add to bean sprouts. Keep cold. Seafoods can be added for a change, such as shrimps, crab, Japanese *hokki* clams (these are fantastic pinkish-white large clams with a texture similar to abalone), abalone and so on. Carrots and white Japanese icicle radish *(daikon)* grated on a fairly large grater cutter make nice additions. (Be sure to salt these additional vegetables first to remove excess liquid from them.) Soaking a few dried mushrooms for 20 minutes and then squeezing out water and cutting into thin strips makes a nice addition, too. This is a most refreshing salad and springlike in appearance. Do not substitute canned bean sprouts for the fresh ones.

Oriental Salad Dressing

Mix 3 Tbsp. rice wine vinegar or lemon juice, dash of MSG, 3 Tbsp. soy and 1 Tbsp. sugar. Add 2 Tbsp. oil very slowly. Stir constantly. Use with cucumbers, cabbage, lettuce, tomatoes or any other salad vegetable. Delicious on bits of meat, too. Try 1 tsp. grated ginger for more flavor and zip!

Celery and Crab Sunomono (Japanese)

Remove strings from 2 or 3 ribs of celery. Cut into 2-inch julienne, thin lengths. Soak in water for 10 minutes. Drain. Take 1 cucumber, sliced thin, and sprinkle lightly with salt. Let stand for 5 minutes. Squeeze out excess water. Combine with 1 can crab, boned and shredded. Make a dressing of ½ cup rice wine vinegar, 1 tsp. soy, 1 tsp. salt, 3 Tbsp. sugar and ¼ tsp. MSG. Mix well with all ingredients for salad. You may wish to reduce vinegar quantity.

Cucumber Salad (Japanese)

The Japanese have a theory that, if you cut off one end of the cucumber and rub it vigorously at the tip, it will remove the bitterness in its entirety. It has not proven so in practice for me. I can see the foam or *aku* (Japanese) oozing out but the cucumber is often still bitter for me. So, I just cut a piece and taste it. If it is bitter, I discard it. Why spoil the entire dish? Maybe you know a sure fire method that may work for you? I do believe in the late growing season it is more likely to be "bitterish"!

3 cups very thinly sliced cucumbers	3 Tbsp. vinegar (rice vinegar preferred)
½ tsp. salt	3 Tbsp. sugar
1 tsp. finely chopped ginger	dash MSG

Partially peel cucumbers, leaving strips of green and slice very thin. Add salt to cucumbers and let stand for 15 minutes. Combine remaining ingredients. Squeeze excess liquid from cucumbers. Drain. Add cucumbers to sauce. Chill and serve as relish or salad. Add the finely chopped ginger. Thinly sliced raw mushrooms, carrots or abalone (cut thin strips) can be added. Freshly cooked shrimp pieces, crab, Japanese *hokki* clams as well as certain types of raw fish (such as sea bass or tuna) that is exceedingly fresh can be added. Thin, sweet red onion slices are nice to add with cucumbers, if desired.

Rice wine vinegar has a certain very mild flavor, but one can substitute regular cider vinegar with a little water to get a similar weak acidity. The flavor, however, will not be quite like the authentic rice wine vinegar.

AEMONO SALAD SAUCES (JAPANESE)

The dressing sauces for *aemono* are heavier and poured over the vegetables as compared to *sunomono* types which are thin and vinegary and the vegetables are mixed with the sauce.

We can beautifully adapt this *aemono* idea for wonderful *hors d'oeuvres* American-style as well as a different salad for your regular menus. Most of them are fairly low in oils and flavorsome. Generally, in Japan they are served in small quantities artistically arranged on a delicate, dainty ceramic bowl—a dab of this and a dab of that. The Japanese hardly use enough to get much of a taste—so here in America, I usually put the vegetable in a large serving bowl or platter and let everyone help themselves to as much as they wish to eat.

Sumiso—Velvety Sauce (Japanese)

When I first introduced this mixture in my many classes years ago, the students actually cleaned out grocery shelves of *miso* (soy bean paste)—the first time the Oriental foods industry had sales runs of such a specialized ingredient! Americans have become so very daring and fearless in venturing into Oriental foods. Some of the very unusual food items would truly "skyrocket" anybody with their peculiar smells, their odd textures and general unfamiliar character. But basically the Orientals have been surviving on them for centuries. We in America are getting very cultivated taste buds and we know what is tasty!

5 Tbsp. *miso* (Japanese white soy bean paste—*shiro miso*)	½ tsp. MSG
4 Tbsp. rice wine vinegar	4 Tbsp. sugar

Cream the white *miso* in *suribachi* (Japanese bowl) if available, otherwise you can use a blender. Add remaining ingredients. Mix well. Spoon this sauce over parboiled green onions or whatever vegetable you decide to use. Garnish with toasted sesame seeds, if desired.

I strongly advise purchasing the soy bean paste (*shiro miso shinshu* type imported from Japan). The flavor is mild and most compatible with American taste buds. Usually comes packed in a cottage-cheese like container in a plastic bag. The paste keeps indefinitely if well-covered in the refrigerator. I do suggest you use it up within a 6 months' period. This sauce is especially excellent poured over parboiled cauliflower, carrots, broccoli, asparagus spears, *nappa* cabbage or whatever you would like to try, even raw tomatoes or cucumbers. Parboil the green onions, for instance, in boiling water for about 3 minutes. Should still be very crisp-tender. Drain. Pass cold water through the hot vegetable. Drain. Squeeze excess water out and place the green onions in neat order—roots all at one end and slice in 1½-inch lengths. Arrange carefully on platter. Pour *sumiso* over the vegetable.

Parboil all vegetables very slightly and always keep them crisp and underdone by American standards. Seafoods have an affinity for this special sauce. Try *hokki* clams—a Japanese clam that can be purchased in flat, round cans. These are ivory-colored clams with tinges of faint pink and very large, about the size of a silver dollar, similar to abalone in texture.

String Beans Aemono (Japanese)

½ lb. fresh string beans, boiled rapidly in salted water for just a few minutes until just tender and still crunchy. Cool quickly under cold water tap. Drain. Cut string beans into 1½-inch lengths. Place neatly in rows on plate. Make the following sauce: ¼ cup roasted peanuts (Virginia style without thin skins), chop and grind well. Mix with 1½ Tbsp. sugar, 2 Tbsp. soy, and dash of MSG. Pour on top of vegetables. Dried bonito fish shavings could be used as garnish.

Vegetables—Served as Side Dishes (Japanese)

Wash 1 good-sized bunch of fresh spinach well. Keep the stem end on. Place in a pan with the stem down in boiling water. No salt necessary. Cook about 3 minutes over high heat until the upper leaves begin to wilt. The color should be a very bright green. Drain. Run under cold water to stop the cooking process. Arrange neatly lengthwise. Trim some of the root section and cut into 2-inch lengths. Spinach should be quite firm and not soft. Squeeze excess water out. Place cut spinach upright in a serving bowl. Serve with any of these sauces:

SWEET SOY SAUCE (JAPANESE):

2 Tbsp. soy	dash of MSG
2 Tbsp. sugar	

Mix together well to dissolve sugar. Pour over cold spinach. Sprinkle with toasted black sesame seeds.

SWEET AND SOUR SESAME SAUCE (JAPANESE):

3 Tbsp. sesame seeds, toasted and partially ground	1 Tbsp. soy
3 Tbsp. sugar	1 tsp. salt
3 Tbsp. rice wine vinegar	½ tsp. MSG

Combine all ingredients and mix well. May be used on our American-style tossed greens, Japanese-style vegetable preparations or whatever your imagination devises. I know some people who pour it over hot rice.

Optional vegetables: Parboiled asparagus, celery, celery root, string beans, watercress (raw), *nappa* cabbage, and so on. Most of these can be parboiled, although, it does go well with certain raw vegetables. Keep experimenting.

Additional Vegetables and Ingredients Guide

*Bamboo shoots—crisp, ivory colored vegetable usually canned. Keeps up to five days in refrigerator. Change water frequently to prevent souring. Does not freeze well.

*Bitter melon—balsam pear—appearance like a grooved wrinkled cucumber. Dark green and very bitter. Almost like a tonic. Contains quinine. Sliced and used in stir-fried or stuffed dishes. Parboil 5 minutes if you wish to reduce bitterness.

Bok choy—Chinese chard—like Swiss chard but far more delicate. Cook 2-3 minutes only.

*Burdock (*gobo*)—long slender brown roots used for Japanese cookery especially.

*Chinese parsley—fresh coriander or often sold as *cilantro* (Latin name). Never substitute regular parsley. Keeps well in plastic container in ice box. Omit, if unavailable. Can be grown from untreated inexpensive coriander seeds from your grocer's spice rack. Do not get fancy quality—they are treated so they will not sprout.

Daikon—white, long icicle-type radish. Originally from the Orient.

*Fuzzy melon or squash *(mo gwa)*—like a fat avocado with

hair fuzz all over surface. A good substitute would be small size summer or zucchini squash.

Jicama—commonly used in Mexican cookery and in Hawaii. Pronounced *hicama.* Tropical root vegetable similar in appearance to a giant rutabaga. Good substitute for water chestnuts—crisp and crunchy.

Nappa or celery cabbage or Chinese cabbage is not really celery or cabbage. More like a lettuce-type vegetable. Very mild and used raw in salads or cooked like spinach or combined in entrees. Keep crisp and undercooked.

Shungiku—edible garland chrysanthemum plant. Used as vegetable in *sukiyaki, tempura,* and other Oriental dishes both by Japanese and by Chinese. Substitute watercress or spinach although *shungiku* has a definite distinctive flavor.

Water chestnuts (caltrops)—brown bulbs size of walnuts with dark rough skin. Fresh ones are especially delicious and crunchy. Tastes like sweet coconut raw, or add to cooked dishes. Both canned or fresh ones freeze well.

Wintermelon—dark green powdery, dusty looking skin. Looks like watermelon. Flesh is white and sweet tasting. Used for soups and in entrees.

Five spices—a blend of cinnamon, anise, fennel, cloves and Chinese pepper. Americans find this a most agreeable flavoring, even for cookies, not just Chinese cooking.

Hoisin sauce—sweet vegetable sauce—dark, brownish brick colored sweet spicy sauce. Used as a condiment as well as for cooking flavor.

MSG—monosodium glutamate is a natural seasoning derivative from wheat, sugar beets and other natural plant sources. Flavor enhancer and in small quantities it has proven harmless.

Mustard paste as served for dips with Chinese meals is simply made with powdered strong dry yellow mustard well mixed with warm water to a smooth creamy paste. You can mix a bit of oil, some brown sugar, a touch of vinegar and soy to make this dipping sauce more authentic.

Nam yoy—red bean curd made from fermented aged bean curd squares, liquor and spices. A true Oriental "cheese."

*Oriental pepper (*sansho* in Japanese and *Szechwan* pepper in Chinese)—not really a pepper. Delicate, fragrant and not hot. Prepared from dehydrated leaves and brown peppercorns of *zanthoxylum piperitum* shrubs. Fresh leaves used for garnish especially by the Japanese.

*Oyster sauce—used as condiment like catsup as well as for cooking. Very little fishy taste. Imparts that special Chinese flavor.

*Soy bean paste—(*miso*). All kinds of varieties on market—dark brown, red and so-called white that looks beige. I prefer the white for consistently mild and not such pungent flavor for Americans.

*Soy bean condiment or soy bean sauce is similar to Japanese *miso* but more potent and imparts entirely a different flavor. Do not substitute this for *miso* in Japanese dishes but you can substitute *miso* for Chinese dishes to a limited degree.

*Soy sauce (*shoyu* or *soya*)—all purpose light Japanese-type for general cooking and table used in recipes in this book. Variations in saltiness, so taste before serving. Chinese-types are far saltier so use less soy than recipe calls for. Do not use soy sauce manufactured in the United States. Does not resemble real soy in flavor.

*Star anise is dark brown star-shaped spice with licorice flavor.

Wasabi—Japanese green-colored horseradish. Available in America in canned powdered form. Mix with cold water and use as condiment. Excellent mixed with sour cream or mayonnaise for American table use.

*Wines:

Sake—Japanese rice wine. Although *sake* can be partaken at room temperature, it is at its best when served slightly warmed with meals.

*Use sherry for general cooking. Any white wine is satisfactory—whiskey, gin, rice wine (*sake*) or even flat champagne could be substituted.

Mirin—Japanese glutinous sweet rice wine used for Japanese cooking. Has sugar added.

POULTRY DISHES

Chinese Chicken Salad

1 chicken fryer, about 2½ to 3 lbs. (select as lean as you can)
1 head of iceberg lettuce
Chinese parsley (fresh coriander)
2 Tbsp. sesame seeds, toasted (or almonds, cashews, peanuts, macadamias, toasted and chopped)
2 oz. rice sticks, deep-fried (*mai fun*). The type packed in 1-inch diameter bunches and about 5 inches long is the easiest to handle. Separate carefully and drop into hot, deep fat, 350°F. Be prepared for the "explosion" that mushrooms up. Remove instantly to drain on paper towels. A fantastic substitute for the fried rice sticks is several handfuls of coarsely crushed potato chips!

Ingredients for sauce mixed in a small bowl:

4 Tbsp. soy
2 Tbsp. honey (clover, preferred)
dash of MSG
1 clove garlic, crushed
1 tsp. salt

Ingredients for sauce mixed in small pan

2 or 3 Tbsp. oil
2 green onions, slivered
½ tsp. grated ginger
several dashes of pepper

Wash and clean chicken. Boil a large pot of unsalted water. Put in the whole (uncut) chicken. After it comes to a boil, lower heat and simmer for 15 minutes. Turn off flame and let chicken cool in water for another 20 minutes. Remove from pot and place on a dish to cool enough so you can handle it. Take out all the bones and remove whatever skin is too thick and fatty.

Note: When you remove chicken from pot, if there is still blood in the thigh area, replace in pot and simmer another 5 minutes more. Cool in pan a short while. Then proceed as above.

Place in the refrigerator.

Wash and arrange shredded lettuce in deep bowl. Cut the cold chicken into small pieces and place on top of lettuce.

Put rice sticks on top of chicken so that all the chicken will not be completely submerged. Pour warm sauce over entire salad. Garnish with toasted seeds or nuts and chopped Chinese parsley. Toss just before serving.

Prepare sauce in this manner. Allow bowl ingredients to stand a few minutes. Heat the small pan ingredients over a low flame for 2 minutes. Pour this into bowl ingredients. Mix well. Remove garlic clove and discard. Sauce is now ready for the salad.

This is not a salad as we know salad. It is more of a chicken entree with lettuce shreds—a really different way to prepare a chicken salad. It has a lot less calories than mixing with mayonnaise American-style, and much more intriguing flavors, too.

Make a few chickens while you are at it and freeze them ready for use. Condense broth and save for soup or stock. This is an easy salad for luncheons or in the summer time when you do not especially wish to cook. The chicken made up this way and packed down into small containers and frozen makes the most wonderful chicken slices for sandwiches or for a cold-cuts platter. If you know that you are using the chicken for purposes other than the above salad, then flavor the chicken with salt, MSG and whatever seasonings that you prefer at the time of simmering.

Heavenly Chicken Wings (Chinese)

Such a mundane part of the chicken—who would go to the trouble of using them? The Chinese have found more ways to use the wings than one could ever imagine!

Drumsticks Made From Chicken Wings

Here's an excellent way to stretch your budget in a tasty manner. Select about 2 lbs. chicken wings. Cut into 3 sections at the joints. See Figure #1. Discard the tip or save for soup stock. You could have a container in the freezer and keep stash-

ing away chicken bones, wing tips, and so on until you have
enough accumulated for making soup stock.

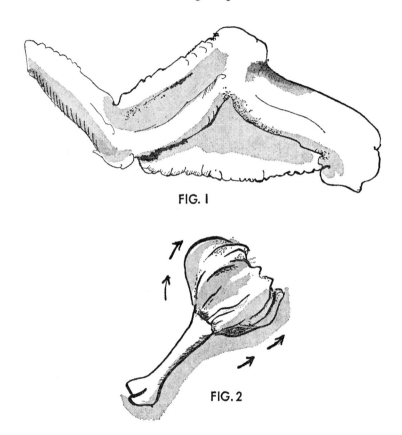

FIG. I

FIG. 2

With a thin, sharp paring knife, cut the tissues that secure
the meat to the bone at the knobby base of the upper section
of the wing. See Figure #2. Push meat upwards so that the
meat is shoved to the opposite end. Flip this meat that has been
loosened at the bottom over the top section. Keep working at it
until it forms a cover like a drumstick. The inside part gets
inverted to the outside. Takes practice and patience, but worth
the effort.

Marinate in:

1 Tbsp. soy	1 Tbsp. sherry
½ tsp. grated ginger	dash of salt
	dash of MSG

Soak 20 minutes or longer. Roll in cornstarch (or water chestnut flour). Steam for 10 minutes to firm up the batter coating. Cool. Deep-fry quickly. Be sure inside gets cooked thoroughly. Make a sweet and sour sauce and use as a dip or pour over the fried wings. Pineapple chunks, maraschino cherries or assorted vegetable chunks could be added to the sauce for color, if desired.

Sweet and Sour Sauce

1 tsp. soy	3 Tbsp. vinegar
1 Tbsp. cornstarch	dash of MSG
4 Tbsp. sugar	2 Tbsp. catsup
	½ cup pineapple juice or water

Mix all ingredients in sauce pan and cook to thicken. Increase to 1½ Tbsp. cornstarch if you desire a heavier dipping sauce. Stir constantly. If fruits or vegetables are added, do so now. Cook a few minutes, but retain the crisp-tender quality. Use as a dipping sauce or pour over the fried miniature chicken "drumsticks." Arranged on a platter lined with a thin layer of shredded lettuce it makes an exotic dish.

Stuffed Boneless Wings

Chop off the 2 bone ends of the mid-section of the chicken wing. See Figure #3. In order to make this boneless, stand piece on the table edge and with the pressure of thumb nails and fingers work the flesh downwards to expose two bones. Turn over and do the same to the other side. The two little bones will now come out very easily. Fill the cavity left by the bones with the filling for Stuffed Green Peppers (p. 169). The chicken will transform miraculously into a triangular shape. Proceed to fry in pan to brown. Add a little water to help steam chicken. Cover and steam-fry for 15 minutes. Pour on black bean sauce (see recipe under Stuffed Green Peppers p. 170) over the cooked wings. Garnish with shredded green onions and Chinese parsley sprigs.

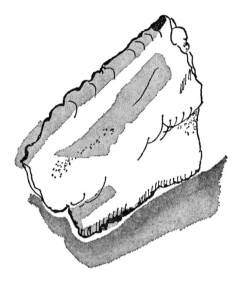

FIG. 3

VARIATIONS:

Fill the cavity with strips of ham, pork or vegetables, cut into julienne strips. Use firm vegetables such as carrots, bamboo shoots, string beans (leave them as is and use), celery or make up your own combinations. You can prepare these stuffed wing sections steamed and sautéed, battered and deep-fried with various sauces or whatever your ingenuity dictates. You can adapt this method of raw chicken preparation to your southern fried style, too. Since this is a tedious preparation process, make up about 5 lbs. of wings at one time and freeze what you do not use for future needs. Make a batch of drumsticks, boned and stuffed wings, and a container full of wing tips for soup.

Fried Boneless Chicken With Nuts (Chinese)

Skin and bone large fryer about 3 lbs. Cut into bite-size pieces.
Marinate in:

2 Tbsp. soy
1 tsp. sugar
1 Tbsp. sherry
1 tsp. grated ginger
1 tsp. *hoisin* sauce
¼ tsp. heavy soy or heavy

molasses (optional), only
   for color
1 clove garlic, minced
   a few drops of sesame oil
1 tsp. salt

Soak chicken in marinade for 30 minutes or more. Remove
and dip chicken in batter mixture of 2 eggs, beaten, ½ cup
cornstarch and ½ cup flour. Fry in deep-fat 350°F. until golden
brown. Line a deep platter with shredded lettuce. Place chicken
on lettuce. Garnish with sprigs of Chinese parsley, a wedge of
lemon and sliced tomatoes. Sprinkle with 1 cup nuts, chopped
or crushed like powder. Use peanuts, cashews, walnuts or
macadamia nuts.

Chicken Balls (Japanese)

1 lb. ground raw chicken meat
   —thigh portion very good
6 dried mushrooms, softened
   in water, squeezed dry
   and minced
3 green onions, minced
2 carrots, or ½ cup frozen
   peas boiled, drained and
   minced

1½ Tbsp. sherry
1 or 1½ Tbsp. soy
1 tsp. sugar
½ tsp. salt
1 egg
   dash of MSG
1½ Tbsp. cornstarch
4 Tbsp. green *nori* seaweed
   (about 1 sheet of seaweed)

Place all ingredients except the seaweed in a bowl and mix
well. Form balls about ¾ inch in diameter and fry in small
quantity of oil. Fry long enough (about 15 minutes) so the
cornstarch will be cooked. A coating of cornstarch often helps
to keep the shape of the balls more intact. You could keep cover
on pan for part of the cooking period. Electric skillet is ideal
since it rarely burns food that is being fried. When done, place
on a platter and sprinkle coarsely torn pieces of green *nori* seaweed on the balls, if desired.

Toasting the seaweed prior to using crisps it nicely and brings out a good flavor. To toast *nori* pass over a gas flame or electric burner on medium high. Do this a few times and the heat will remove any excess moisture in the seaweed. It can also be toasted in the oven for a brief period.

VARIATIONS:

Make like hamburger patties and fry. Or place on one dish and steam for 15 minutes for a different appearing entree. With a good coating of cornstarch, the little balls can be deep-fried in hot oil. This makes a good appetizer.

Tossed Shredded Chicken Salad (Chinese)

Marinate 2 uncooked chicken breasts for 1 hour in ¼ cup soy, 1 clove garlic, minced, 1 tsp. sherry wine, ½ tsp. sugar, dash of MSG and ½ tsp. grated ginger. Deep-fry chicken breasts in hot oil until golden brown. Be sure they are cooked all the way through. Cool. Remove chicken meat and shred.

Now marinate cooked chicken in the following seasonings:

1 tsp. sesame oil	¼ tsp. 5-spice powder
¾ tsp. to 1 tsp. salt	¼ tsp. sugar
½ tsp. pepper	dash of MSG
1 tsp. dry mustard	

Prepare the following and toss with chicken just before serving.

½ head of lettuce, thinly shredded or about 12-14 leaves (about 2 cups)	¼ cup Chinese parsley, cut in short lengths
4 green onions, shredded in 1½-inch lengths	1 oz. rice sticks (*mai fun*), deep-fried, and broken into small pieces

Garnish with ⅓ cup salted peanuts, chopped (or use toasted sesame seeds or toasted slivered almonds).

One can increase or decrease flavorings to taste. This salad is served as an entree and can be served slightly warm by keeping the chicken and marinade heated until serving time.

Chicken With Cashews (Chinese)

2 cups chicken, sliced into thin strips—½ inch by 1½ inches or ½-inch cubes (use one fryer or 2 whole chicken breasts). Marinate with the following:

1 Tbsp. soy	½ cup onions, diced
1 Tbsp. cornstarch	1 cup bamboo shoots, diced or
1 Tbsp. sherry	½ cup bamboo and ½
½ tsp. MSG	cup water chestnuts
1 clove garlic, minced	½ cup celery, diced
1 tsp. ginger, grated	1 cup fresh mushrooms, diced
½ tsp. salt, more or less	1 pkg. thawed frozen peas or
Add 1 Tbsp. oil to coat above	⅓ lb. Chinese fresh edible-
cornstarch and chicken	pod peas, diced
mixture to prevent sticking	

GRAVY:

1 Tbsp. soy	¾ cup water or chicken stock
1 Tbsp. cornstarch	1 cup salted cashew nuts, pine-
½ tsp. sugar	nuts or almonds

Toss-fry onions, bamboo shoots, celery, water chestnuts (if used) and peas with 1 Tbsp. oil over high heat for 1 minute; remove from pan. Toss-fry the mushrooms with ½ Tbsp. oil over high heat for 10 seconds. Add to the vegetables. Toss-fry marinated chicken in 1 Tbsp. oil over high heat until whitish, scraping pan as you toss-fry to prevent sticking. Add vegetables and the gravy ingredients. Cook until thickened. Adjust seasonings, if necessary. Garnish with warmed-up nuts (place in oven for short period to heat through). Serve piping hot. Raw cashew or peanuts are authentic to use in Chinese cooking and are available in certain Oriental shops as well as in many health food stores. I find vacuum packed nuts to be excellent and they simplify the many steps involved in Chinese-style cooking. If using raw nuts be sure and sauté in oil or deep-fry first before using.

Deep-Fried Crispy Chicken (Chinese)

Cut up a 3-lb. chicken fryer in quarters. Mix and brush on all areas the following seasonings which have been mixed together:

1 tsp. salt or more	1 tsp. grated ginger
dash MSG	1 clove garlic, minced
dash sugar	2 Tbsp. soy
2 Tbsp. sherry	

Put cornstarch in a plastic bag and shake your large pieces of seasoned chicken quarters in it. Deep-fry at 350°F. for 10 minutes on each side. Allow plenty of room, otherwise, they will not get cooked fast enough and the chicken will have a tendency to be greasy. Use your Chinese brass skimmer to lift and drain oil. Chop into serving pieces. Garnish with chopped green onions and Chinese parsley. Serve hot.

Five-Spices Roast Chicken (Chinese)

2½ to 3-lb. chicken fryer, whole or split down the back	¼ of an onion, chopped dashes of sugar and salt
2 Tbsp. honey	1 tsp. of 5-spices
2 Tbsp. soy	dash of black pepper
1 clove garlic, minced	Chinese parsley, chopped
1 tsp. grated ginger	1 Tbsp. sherry
½ tsp. MSG	

Marinate chicken in soy and honey mixed with the onion, sugar, salt, garlic, Chinese parsley, a pinch of 5-spices, ginger, MSG and sherry for a few hours or overnight. Turn over occasionally so marinade will penetrate all surfaces. Arrange the chicken on baking pan with the skin side up or the breast side up as the case may be. Mix the remainder of the 5-spices and black pepper and sprinkle on the chicken. A little 5-spices goes a long way so use it sparingly.

Roast at 325°F. for 45-60 minutes. Should be deep golden brown. If whole chicken is used, turn over once during the roasting process. Can be served hot or cold. Gravy could be thickened or left thin. Garnish with chopped Chinese parsley. Serve roast chicken chopped into serving pieces (bones and all). This chicken is fine for a picnic lunch. Goes well with Japanese rice balls. At one church dinner, one of my students supervised the preparation of this chicken for 600 persons. It was a most successful church social event!

Sweet and Sour Chicken (Chinese)

1 chicken fryer, 2½ to 3 lbs. or substitute breasts and thighs	½ green pepper, cut into big chunks
1 or 2 eggs	1 large onion, cut into big chunks, separated
cornstarch	1 can pineapple chunks

MARINADE:

1 Tbsp. sherry	1 tsp. grated ginger
1 Tbsp. soy	½ tsp. MSG
1 clove garlic, minced	1 tsp. salt

Cut chicken into bite-size pieces and marinate for 2 hours or more in the marinade mixture. Stir occasionally.

Break the egg or two into the chicken marinating bowl. Stir. Add enough cornstarch cautiously to make a sticky batter. About ½ cup will be right, but this depends upon the size of the eggs and you may need more. Too much will cement the pieces and you'll find you cannot even begin to stir! One of my students put too much cornstarch, so tried to remedy it by adding more egg, then more cornstarch and so on. I do not know how she came out of the home cement-mixer at the right consistency.

Heat oil in electric skillet. You can fry this with only about ½ inch of oil or less, or deep-fry in more oil. I personally prefer the small amount of oil. Brown nicely and drain. Meanwhile, make the sauce. If the pieces are very large, you can finish cooking by putting the browned chicken in a 325°F. oven for about 10 to 15 minutes to complete the cooking.

SAUCE:

2 tsp. soy	Juice from canned pineapple plus water to equal about 1 cup liquid
2 Tbsp. cornstarch	
8 Tbsp. sugar	
6 Tbsp. vinegar	dash of MSG
4 Tbsp. catsup	

After the chicken has been browned, clean frying pan, and sauté in 1 Tbsp. oil for 2 minutes the green pepper and onion which have been cut in half crosswise and then each half into chunks. Remove to platter.

Mix sauce ingredients in pan, cook until thickened. Add onion, pepper, pineapple combination to sauce. Heat thoroughly. Put chicken on platter, lined with a bed of shredded lettuce. Pour sauce over chicken.

VARIATIONS:

Use 2 lbs. pork butt cut in ¾-inch cubes. One large can lichee nuts may be used in place of the pineapple. Celery and tomatoes can be substituted for onion and green peppers.

An exciting garnish for this dish is a handful or two of cocktail peanuts, chopped, and green onions, slivered.

This fried chicken freezes very nicely. Defrost and warm up in oven. Make the sauce just before serving since there is less chance for it to get watery.

Chicken in Papers (Chinese)

3 cups chicken meat, cut into small pieces (bite-size).
   Marinate in the following:

2 Tbsp. oil	½ tsp. sugar
1 Tbsp. soy	2 Tbsp. green onions, chopped
1 Tbsp. worcestershire sauce	2 Tbsp. Chinese parsley,
1 Tbsp. sherry	chopped
1 Tbsp. *hoisin* sauce (red	1 clove garlic, minced
bean sauce or vegetable	1½ Tbsp. cornstarch
sauce)	dash salt
1 tsp. sesame oil	dash MSG

For a slightly milder taste, you can eliminate the worcestershire sauce, *hoisin* sauce, and Chinese parsley from the above marinade.

Cut parchment-type paper into 4-inch squares. You will need about 50 for this recipe, more or less. Wax paper, such as the butcher uses, is ideal since it is heavily coated and more impregnated with waterproofing material—more like a glassine paper. Regular wax paper as used in our kitchens to wrap sandwiches, aluminum foil, parchment typing paper and similar materials could be used.

Place 1 Tbsp. marinated chicken mixture in one piece of

paper and fold envelope wrap. Please refer to the section "Oriental Envelope Wrap" for directions. Fry in deep-fat 350°F. for about 3 minutes until done. It is a good idea to fry packages with the flap side down first. Then, turn over and fry a few more seconds. Drain on paper towels. Serve piping hot! Do not eat this paper, unwrap and sort of munch at the delectable morsels stuck on the paper.

If you desire a more low-calorie method of preparation, line the packets as you make them on a cookie sheet. Bake them at 425°F. oven for 15 minutes. Packet will become rather tan looking. This is the closest to the deep-fried type in flavor, without any greasiness. I like this special method the best myself. These little treats are a wonderful addition to any meal or they can be used as hors d'oeuvres.

Foil-wrapped packets can be baked at 500°F. for 10 minutes. The flavor is a bit different from the deep-fried paper wrapped ones, more of a steamed flavor, but still good. You can also deep-fry these foil wrapped packets. Do them the same as the paper wrapped manner.

Chinese Peking Duck

If you are near one of the large Chinese communities in the United States, you can purchase Chinese-style marinated roasted ducks. They are very deeply browned and so succulent! They are dangling in the food shops looking so curiously different from what we see in our regular delicatessens. There is a head still attached. The glossy skin is crisp and brittle.

Once, when I purchased one for home, my young son was so amazed to see a duck's head in the container he had to save it in the refrigerator to bring to school for "show and tell." Definitely, children these days are not growing up with the familiar inhabitants we took for granted in rural America—like a duck waddling up to you quacking and wiggling its stubby tail!

Simply place the duck in a baking pan, first cutting off the head. You could be fancy and free the skin away from the body and so on, but be practical and just warm the duck. Bake about

25-30 minutes in a 325°F. oven, just to heat through the whole duck. Allow extra time if it is icy-cold when put into the oven.

Remove the wooden skewers from the duck. Pour out any juices that might still remain in the body of the duck. Put duck on platter and keep warm. Skim off from the juices all the fat that you can. Add some water to make the juices and water equal about ¾ cup liquid. Blend in 1 Tbsp. cornstarch dissolved in a little water. Cook and stir until thickened. You may wish to increase the cornstarch a bit.

Serve the duck carved in small pieces. The skin is especially delicious and prized. You could serve plain duck along with various other entrees that you have prepared. It adds a certain something to any Oriental meal. Or, you could make some yeast rolls (like Parker House rolls) and steam them (as a substitute, use flour *tortillas*). As condiments have dishes of *hoisin* sauce, Chinese parsley sprigs, green onions, slivered, and some shredded lettuce. Serve the gravy, also. To eat, put some duck into the buns and add your desired embellishments.

USES FOR LEFTOVER PEKING DUCK—IF
YOU HAVE ANY REMAINING!

The leftover meat and juices can be used to make a base for a meal. Add, perhaps some bean sprouts and toss-fry. Add more seasonings, if desired. Or, cut up some bean curd into 1-inch cubes, along with some green onions, chopped, and heat through with the leftover duck. With hot rice this can be a most satisfactory and delicious meal. You could put Chinese cabbage (*nappa*) or whatever you wish to create your own thing. This Peking duck flavor is so magnificent, it's an extravagance not to eat every juicy morsel! Adding a few sprigs of Chinese parsley for garnish as well as for flavor makes for increased pleasure. And, with the head, the carcass and whatever else you might have, such as a pork bone or two, you can make a delightful soup base with perhaps some Chinese cabbage (*nappa*) added. Garnish with green onion slivers and Chinese parsley.

This duck freezes nicely so buy a few extras. They are worth the relatively high cost since one cannot duplicate this type of cooking very easily at home. I especially stress getting one that has been freshly roasted or one which has been in freezer storage a very brief while. There is a tendency for highly spiced foods to lose some of their flavor when stored too long. By long, I refer to over 3-4 months for poultry.

Turkey With Oriental Flavors

You would not find turkey native to the Orient—but here in America it is so plentiful that these days one just does not reserve it for Thanksgiving Day alone. Instead of the usual flavor perk it up this way!

1 hen turkey (fresh, if possible) about 12 lbs. (if fresh frozen, I do like the one with the automatic timer inserted in the body of the turkey, which pops out at the exact time the fowl is done to perfection. It is marvelous and certainly beats poking here and there to see if it is done or not.)

SEASONINGS: MIX ALL OF THIS IN A BOWL

2 Tbsp. salt
2 Tbsp. soy
4 Tbsp. oil
½ tsp. MSG
1 clove garlic, minced

½ tsp. ginger, grated
2 Tbsp. Chinese parsley, chopped
dash of 5-spices

DRESSING FOR THE TURKEY:

1 lb. fairly lean sausage meat or use 12 oz. package of "brown and serve" pork sausages, chopped
2 slices of cooked ham, chopped
1 celery rib, chopped
1 onion, chopped
1 to 2 cups fresh mushrooms, chopped

½ to 1 tsp. salt (adjust to taste)
1 tsp. soy
dash of sugar and MSG
2 cups raw, long-grain rice which has been cooked ahead and allowed to become cold (equals about 4 or 5 cups cooked rice). Refrigerated rice is best.

Sauté the sausage and drain excess oil. Add the ham and stir-fry a minute or so. Add the onion, celery and mushrooms. Stir to mix. Now, blend in the salt, soy, sugar and MSG. Cook for about 3 minutes for the vegetables to soften somewhat. Add the cold rice. Toss-fry to separate the grains. Adjust the flavorings to your taste. This is almost a fried rice combination. Cool the mixture.

Wash the turkey, drain and dry well. Rub the inside and the outside of the turkey with salt. Stuff the turkey lightly and use skewers to hold the openings closed. You will have some dressing left over, so place it in a covered casserole and put it in the oven to cook through about 30 minutes before serving. Baste with some of the turkey juices occasionally to flavor. Tie the legs together so that they will not spring up in the roasting process. Do likewise with the wings if the pan does not hold them in place. Take a pastry brush and paint the seasonings mixture on the outside of the turkey. Try to get all the area so that the coloring will be evenly distributed. Roast at 325°F. for about 3½ hours. Baste periodically with the juices that collect in the pan.

Simmer the giblets in 1 quart of water with a piece of celery, onion and salt for 1½ hours while the turkey roasts.

When done remove the turkey to a serving platter and let rest for 15 to 20 minutes before carving. This sets the meat and makes it much easier to carve. Make a gravy with the giblets that were simmered ahead of time. Use the familiar gravy-making method of flour browned in the pan and the turkey stock added slowly. Cook until thickened. Adjust seasonings but remember that there is a lot of salt and other flavorings in the pan drippings.

Crisp Cornish Game Hen (Chinese)

3 whole Cornish game hens	dash of 5-spices (optional)
1 clove garlic, minced	1 tsp. salt
3 Tbsp. soy	¼ tsp. MSG
1 Tbsp. sherry	⅛ tsp. pepper
1 Tbsp. brown sugar	1 tsp. grated ginger
Chinese parsley, chopped	½ cup cornstarch

GLAZE:

2 Tbsp. honey	2 Tbsp. soy

Marinate the birds for 2 hours or longer in all the ingredients except for the cornstarch and the glaze. Turn occasionally so marinade will cover entire bird. Put a dab inside of the bird. Put hens and marinade in a deep cake pan or bowl. Place on a rack in your steamer. Steam for 40 minutes turning the hens over once so that they will be in the marinade on both the back and the breast side. Remove from steamer. Dry birds off. Save juices for gravy. Brush hens with the above glaze of honey and soy. Let stand 20 minutes to cool. Brush again with glaze if any dribbled onto pan. I save any leftover glaze and add it to the gravy for extra flavor. Mix about ½ cup cornstarch and a dash of salt. (You may need more cornstarch.) Pat on the wet, glazed hens. Allow to stand 15-20 minutes. Place on a plate and steam for 10 minutes or a bit longer for the cornstarch to set. Cool.

Heat 2 inches of oil in a deep skillet or *wok*. Deep-fry hens one at a time until golden brown, turning often. This does not take more than a few minutes at a time on each side. Keep rolling the hen in pan so that the browning will be even. A Chinese brass skimmer 5 to 7 inches in diameter is excellent for deep-fat frying. And for draining hens as you take them out of the oil.

Place on paper towels to drain. Put on hot platter. Cut into serving pieces or leave whole. Sprinkle with chopped green onions and garnish with Chinese parsley. Make a gravy with the strained juices and glaze drippings reserved from the original steaming process. For about 1 cup of juices, add 1 Tbsp. cornstarch dissolved in a little water. Cook until thickened. Serve gravy in separate dish or pour over Cornish hens before sprinkling the Chinese parsley and the green onions on. Chinese parsley sprig can be put inside of hen cavity while steaming, if desired.

BEEF DISHES

FLANK STEAK

Flank steak is one of the most versatile meats. You may have always thought it was one meat cut that had to be stewed for hours to be fork-tender. You may still cook it that way if you like, but with Oriental-style cuisine, if the meat is USDA choice or good quality, it will cook very fast—in minutes. The secret is high heat and cutting the meat cross-grain to cut the lengths of the fibers very short. Top-sirloin, fillet or rib-eye beef are good substitutes for flank steak. Since every beef has only 2 flanks, I suggest that you buy it when you see it; when you need it, the meat will be in the freezer. I have been accused of getting to the markets early and cleaning out the entire stock of flank steaks! There are times when, I admit, I have bought as many as the butcher would spare.

Flank Steak (Korean)

1 piece of flank steak	2 Tbsp. sherry
¼ cup sugar	dash of pepper and MSG
¼ cup soy (or more)	1 clove garlic, minced
2 stalks chopped green onions	flour
	1 egg, beaten

Flank steak could be tenderized at butcher shop or pound it with the edge of a sturdy saucer. Marinate steak in sugar, soy, sherry, pepper, MSG and garlic for a few hours or more. Coat with flour and dip into egg, then into the chopped green onions. Fry by deep-fat method, very briefly, since you want the center of the steak on the pinkish side. Shred iceberg lettuce on platter. Place steak on the lettuce. Slice across grain to serve a very different steak! True Korean style would dictate you use plenty of cayenne or crushed red chili peppers and garlic—zippy and hot!

Very Special Gold Steak Balls (Chinese)

2 lbs. fillet of beef cut in bite-
size chunks

Marinate for 15 minutes in the following:

½ tsp. grated orange rind (optional and adjust to your
taste)
1 tsp. grated ginger
1 clove minced garlic

2 Tbsp. green onions, minced
1 Tbsp. soy
2 Tbsp. sherry
dashes of sugar and MSG

Spear onto skewers. If you are using your *hibachi,* grill to desired degree of doneness very briefly over hot charcoal. Or you can put in a hot oiled *wok* and sear. Toss-fry a few minutes over the highest heat, should be dry-fried fast!

Garnish platter with a few ribs of Chinese *bok choy* (Chinese chard), cut in 1-inch lengths and sautéed in hot oiled pan for 2 minutes. Toss-fry and season with salt and MSG.

Beef Teriyaki (Japanese)

If you wish to increase this recipe, I would suggest that you make separate bowls of marinade for each batch. There is less flavor change that way.

2 to 3 lbs. top sirloin steak,
flank, eye of rib, sliced ¼
inch thick and about 2 to
2½ inches long
1 or 2 tsp. grated fresh ginger
1 clove garlic, minced

1 medium size onion, chopped
1 tsp. MSG
⅓ cup soy
¼ cup sugar
¼ cup sherry or *sake* or *mirin*

Mix all ingredients and marinate for 1 hour or longer. Drain. Broil 3 to 5 minutes on each side (for beef) over charcoal. The meat can be strung out on skewers for easy handling. One can use the broiler of the stove, if preferred, although the taste is somewhat altered as compared to charcoal broiling.

Green onions cut in 1½-inch lengths, mushroom caps and big chunks of green peppers can be added to the meat if you are putting the strips on skewers. Marinate the vegetables for awhile, too. This makes a Japanese *shish-kabob!*

OPTIONAL METHOD:

Get skillet sizzling hot. Add 1 Tbsp. oil and put the sliced beef in. Toss-fry and stir to brown and sear. Remove to platter. Take the remaining marinade and cook it up a minute or so and pour over meat. Do not overcook.

VARIATIONS:

Use salmon slices, chicken fryer (cut-up), pork steaks, un-shelled shrimps or, even, try turkey.

For chicken, broil one side 10-15 minutes and repeat on other side. Do not overcook, it will be too dry. Can also be baked in the oven at 325°F. for 45 minutes. Test for doneness by poking a skewer in the thick thigh area. Be sure chicken is room temperature when putting in oven or adjust the time allowance.

Spareribs cut into serving pieces may be marinated in *teriyaki* sauce overnight and baked for 2 hours at 325°. Baste ribs occasionally.

Salmon slices broil only about 10 minutes for each side, depending upon thickness. Do not overcook fish. Keep it flaky and moist.

If any marinade is left, use it to cook a few vegetables such as string beans. Remember, however, that there are fresh meat or fish juices intermingled with the marinade so it must be used immediately to prevent spoilage.

Regional taste differences make many people like a stronger soy flavor to *teriyaki*. If so, reduce your sugar somewhat and add more soy. I personally feel too much soy destroys the flavor of the meat. It is quite permissible to add more soy as you eat.

Teppan-Yaki (Japanese)

1 lb. Spencer steaks, fillets, or eye of rib or *sukiyaki* meat cut about ¼ inch thick

2 onions, sliced, about ⅜ inch thick

1 lb. fresh mushrooms, sliced ⅜ inch thick

1 bunch spinach or Chinese *nappa* cabbage, cut in 1-inch lengths

½ lb. bean sprouts

2 bunches green onions, cut into 1½-inch diagonal slices

butter or oil

Heat your electric skillet or griddle to high at the table. Add pat of butter or oil and a portion of meat and vegetables. Arrange the various ingredients separately in nice pattern. Sear the meat and proceed to cook it to your desired degree of doneness. Carefully turn the vegetables over to cook crisp-tender. Be sure to keep each ingredient in its respective place. If necessary, a small cover could be put on top of some of the vegetables for a few minutes to speed the cooking process. Sauté quickly and serve while piping hot. Eat by dipping in a sauce made with ½ cup soy, ½ cup lemon juice or rice wine vinegar, 2 Tbsp. sugar and ½ tsp. MSG. *Alternate sauce*: 2 tsp. dry mustard and 6 Tbsp. soy. Dissolve mustard in small amount of water. Mix with soy. Serve in dipping dishes. Condiments to add to the sauce: chopped green onions, grated ginger, grated Japanese *daikon* radish, crushed sesame seeds and *wabasi* paste, take your choice.

Other meats and vegetables suggested for this mixed barbecue are: oysters, shrimps, scallops, clams on half-shells, chicken meat, watercress, edible-pod peas, green peppers, string beans (Kentucky Wonders are my favorite), small eggplants, summer squash or whatever you wish. This dish would be called *Bata-Yaki* if butter is used for the frying process.

Beef With Tomatoes (Chinese)

2 to 2½ cups flank steak (about 1 to 1¼ lbs. piece), sliced thin, about ¼ inch thick by 2 or 2½ inches wide. Be sure to cut cross grain

2 or 3 firm tomatoes, cut in chunks

2 ribs of celery, cut in chunks diagonally
1 green pepper, cut in chunks
1 onion, cut in chunks
2 stalks of green onion, cut in 1-inch lengths (optional)

Mix in bowl the following seasonings and add the meat Combine all together.

2 Tbsp. soy
½ tsp. sugar
1 Tbsp. sherry
1 Tbsp. cornstarch

1 tsp. ginger, grated
1 clove garlic, minced
dash of pepper and MSG

Add 1 Tbsp. oil after the meat has been mixed with the above Marinate 15 minutes

GRAVY:

¾ tsp. salt	½ tsp. MSG
¾ cup water	1 Tbsp. cornstarch
1 Tbsp. worcestershire sauce	2 Tbsp. catsup
1 tsp. curry (optional)	

The first time you make this recipe, omit curry. Sometimes children do not quite like this seasoning. Get all ingredients prepared. Mix gravy ingredients and put aside. In a very hot skillet, add 1 or 2 Tbsp. oil and toss-fry the meat until partially cooked and slightly pinkish. Remove to another plate. Clean your pan carefully and add more oil when the pan is piping hot. Fry onion, green pepper and celery for 1 minute toss-frying all the while. Add beef. Add gravy ingredients. Toss-fry to thicken gravy. Add tomatoes just to heat through. If green onions are used, add them at this time. Serve piping hot with steamed rice or fried *chow mein* noodles.

Crispy Deep-Fried Beef (Japanese)

2 or 3 lbs. beef like rib eye or tenderloin, sliced ⅛ to ¼ inch thick in strips

Marinate meat in sauce for 2 hours. Mix all ingredients together in bowl.

2 tsp. grated fresh ginger	⅓ cup soy
1 clove garlic, minced	¼ cup sugar
1 medium-size onion, chopped	¼ cup sherry, *sake* or *mirin*
1 tsp. MSG	

Bread marinated beef. (Put beef in some flour, then dip in beaten egg and finally in some fine bread or cracker crumbs.) Set aside for ½ hour to make the crumbs adhere better. Fry in deep-fat 375°F. for 2 minutes until golden brown. Watch carefully since the soy has a tendency to brown very quickly. Drain on paper towels. Excellent hot or cold as an entree or appetizer. Good as sandwich meat, too. Try it cold along with Japanese rice balls for a beach picnic—better than the dull routine sandwiches.

Beef With Broccoli and Oyster Sauce (Chinese)

1⅓ lbs. flank steak (Cut lengthwise down the middle and sliced into thin strips cross grain on a slant—about ¼ inch by 2½ inches)

Marinate and mix meat with the following:

1 Tbsp. soy	1 tsp. sherry
1 Tbsp. cornstarch	salt
½ tsp. MSG	Add 1 Tbsp. oil to coat
1 tsp. grated fresh ginger	above mixture.
4 cups broccoli	

With paring knife peel tough outer skin. Inside sections of stem are all edible! Diagonally slice broccoli into ¼-inch pieces. Partially cut flowerlets from stem area and tear apart into narrower segments with the help of a paring knife.

GRAVY:

1 Tbsp. soy	salt to taste
1 Tbsp. cornstarch	¾ cup water
½ tsp. sugar	2 Tbsp. oyster sauce

Sauté broccoli in hot frying pan over high heat with 1 Tbsp. oil and keep toss-frying for 2 to 3 minutes. Salt. Add a few drops of water, if necessary, to prevent burning. Broccoli should be barely cooked, to keep its bright jade green. Remove from frying pan. Sauté flank steak with 1 Tbsp. oil over high heat until browned. Scrape bottom of pan and keep toss-frying to prevent sticking. While flank steak is still pink in middle, add the precooked broccoli and mixed gravy ingredients. Cook until thickened. Adjust salt since oyster sauces vary in saltiness.

VARIATIONS:

Cauliflower, string beans, asparagus, mushrooms, snow peas (edible-pod), celery, brown onions, bamboo shoots, zucchini squash and Chinese yard-long beans are some of the suggestions. You could even combine several vegetables together. Be sure to use about 1 part of meat to 2 parts of vegetables. Cut vegetables in approximately same size so cooking time will be equal for all slices. This can also be prepared using only meat and garnishing with green onions, chopped. More ginger can be added if you really like ginger flavor. The ginger could be left in ⅛-inch slices, if desired. Do not substitute powdered ginger for the fresh. This could be called "Ginger Beef" if only beef and ginger were the main ingredients.

Chicken and pork can be substituted for the flank steak, although you must be sure the pork is well cooked before adding the vegetables.

Beef in Parchment (Chinese)

3 cups beef (like flank, cut cross-grain or filet mignon), thin, tiny bite-size slices	about ½ inch by ½ inch by ¼ inch or less, or coarsely minced

Marinate meat for 15 minutes or longer:

2 Tbsp. oil	½ tsp. sugar
1 Tbsp. soy	2 Tbsp. chopped green onions
1 Tbsp. worcestershire sauce	2 Tbsp. Chinese parsley, chopped
1 Tbsp. sherry	
1 Tbsp. *hoisin* sauce (red bean sauce or vegetable sauce)	1 clove garlic, minced
	1½ Tbsp. cornstarch
1 tsp. sesame oil	dash of salt and MSG

You will need about 1 lb. *won ton* skins purchased from the store. Toss-fry marinated beef in hot oiled skillet. Cook for about 2 to 3 minutes, should be slightly pink color. Remove to platter. In a clean, hot, oiled pan toss-fry several ribs of *bok choy* (Chinese chard) cut into ½-inch chunks. Add to meat. Blend. Cool. Place 1 Tbsp. beef and green mixture in a *won ton* skin and fold like an envelope. Seal edges well with beaten egg. Fry in deep-fat 350° to 375°F. for about 3 minutes until golden. Fry one side and then turn over to fry a few more seconds. Drain on paper towels. Keep hot in oven on paper towels. Serve piping hot! Serve mustard and soy for dipping. Water chestnut pieces or edible-pod peas, chopped, could be added for variation. Mushrooms, chopped, make a good variation, too. This beef and chard mixture alone can be eaten as an entree without further cooking, with only one difference—toss-fry vegetables and then add precooked meat. Mix and serve.

Snow Over the Mountain (Chinese)

2 cups flank steak (about 1 to 1¼ lbs. meat, cut lengthwise down middle and sliced diagonally into thin ¼-inch by 2-inch strips cross grain.) Substitute sirloin, fillet or rib eye, if desired

Marinate with:

½ tsp. grated ginger
1 Tbsp. soy
1 tsp. sherry

½ tsp. salt
½ tsp. MSG
1 Tbsp. cornstarch

After the meat has been mixed with the marinade add 1 Tbsp. oil.

1 cup Oriental dried mushrooms, soaked in water, squeezed dry before using, cut in thin strips
1 cup celery, cut in thin strips
½ cup onion, cut in thin strips

1 cup edible-pod peas, cut in thin strips or 1 cup fresh string beans, cut in thin strips
2 cups fried rice sticks (*py mai fun*)

GRAVY:

1 Tbsp. cornstarch
1 Tbsp. soy
1 tsp. sugar

½ tsp. MSG
¾ cup water (increase to 1 cup if more gravy desired)

Deep-fry rice sticks. Drain on paper towels. In a very hot frying pan add 1 Tbsp. oil. Sauté marinated beef until pink, toss-frying all the time. Remove from pan. Sauté the mushrooms, celery and onions with 1 Tbsp. oil a few minutes over high heat. Should be only about three-quarters done. Add peas and toss-fry another ½ minute. Salt.

Return beef to pan and add gravy ingredients. Toss together and cook until thickened. Adjust seasonings.

Shred a little iceberg lettuce on platter (optional). Pour meat combination over lettuce. Top with deep-fried rice sticks. This is our "snowfall" on the mountain of meat and vegetables.

This dish is sometimes called "Mock Lamb" or "Wooly Lamb." A variation on this dish is to use only Oriental dried mushrooms (increasing quantity) leaving out the other vegetables. 2 Tbsp. oyster flavored sauce can be added, if desired, along with the gravy ingredients.

PORK DISHES

••

Char Siu—Barbecued Pork (Chinese)

This is, perhaps, my most treasured recipe. It is the sweet fragrant roast pork that everyone finds so irresistible. It will, probably, become a favorite of yours, too.

3 lbs. pork loin or pork butt, cut in ¾ inch to 1 inch thick slices or cut in 1 inch by 1 inch by 4 inch strips

Marinate with:

2 Tbsp. soy
6 Tbsp. brown sugar
2 Tbsp. honey
2 Tbsp. sherry, gin, rum or whiskey
2 Tbsp. *hoisin* sauce (red bean sauce) or you can substitute red bean curd (*nam yoy*). I personally like the combination of 2 Tbsp. *hoisin* sauce and 1 Tbsp.

nam yoy for good authentic flavor.
1 tsp. salt
1 tsp. MSG
¼ tsp. Chinese 5-spices
2 tsp. chopped Chinese parsley
1 clove garlic, minced
½ tsp. grated ginger
½ tsp. saltpeter (optional) or some red food coloring (optional)

Let stand for 2 hours at room temperature or as long as 1 day in the refrigerator before roasting. Flavor is better with longer marinating period. Turn meat occasionally so that it will be well soaked in the marinade. Line a broiler pan with foil. Add hot water to the pan (about half full). Line broiler rack with foil and punch holes for drainage. Put meat on prepared rack. Bake in a preheated oven at 450°F. about 25 minutes for each side. Baste with any remaining marinade in bowl occasionally. Watch carefully since marinade does burn easily.

Alternate method is to hang the pieces of meat with hooks or wires on oven rack over a pan of hot water. The hot water helps to produce a very moist roast and the foil helps to make clean-up a lot simpler. I often do this meat on a large brazier out-of-doors. Spareribs in one slab can be prepared this way, too. Roast for a longer period, about 1¼ hours or more at 400°F. Cut into serving sections to serve. Good hot or cold.

Slice meat diagonally and place on platter. Garnish with Chinese parsley sprigs. Serve with soy and mustard paste. This roast pork can also be used for making steamed buns as well as for garnishes on various foods and it makes wonderful *hors d'oeuvres*. Roast pork freezes very well so be sure to make plenty while you are at it.

DO NOT INCREASE the proportions in this recipe. If you desire to make more, then set bowls out for each portion and make the recipe one time in each bowl. There is a flavor change if doubled and tripled, and so on.

Further hints: Try this recipe with pork chops or pork steaks. Serve everyone a whole chop(s) instead of slicing into pieces. This is an especially good idea when you have hungry people who will forget there are others to share with and gorge themselves if given a chance! It is *that kind* of succulent meat.

Saltpeter from the drug store is not satisfactory for this recipe. It is a different formula. Get yours from the Oriental butcher shops—ask for *char siu salt*. Appearance is like white coarse salt grains. The Chinese use Chilean saltpeter. This saltpeter results in a rich brick-reddish even color throughout for a genuine professional Chinese *char siu*. If not soaked sufficiently, you will be able to detect by the coloration of the cut slices (red ring of color at edges and grey pork meat color towards center), how far the penetration was, so the next time you can marinate longer. The saltpeter does not affect flavor unless overused, so utilize in moderation!

Some interesting notes on saltpeter: saltpeter is not sold very freely since quality control has been under the government's probing eyes. It was used extensively decades ago by butchers to color ground meat to make it look a fresh red. Corned meats, i.e. beef, tongue, pork and ham, all use varying degrees of saltpeter to bring out and retain the reddish color in the curing process.

Sweet and Pungent Pork (Chinese)

Soak together in bowl for 15 minutes or longer

2 lbs. lean pork (butt, loin or leg), cut in ¾-inch cubes	2 eggs, slightly beaten
dash MSG	4 Tbsp. cornstarch
1 clove garlic, minced	½ tsp. salt .
½ tsp. grated ginger	2 tsp. soy
	1 tsp. sherry

Remove pieces of pork from bowl and coat individually with cracker crumbs (or a mixture of half flour and half fine bread crumbs). This is easily done by placing crumbs on a flat pan and rolling meat pieces around. They will automatically be evenly coated. You could use the "plastic bag filled with crumbs and shake" method, but there is tendency for sticky meat chunks to make quite a mess. Allow coating to dry about 15-30 minutes. Deep-fry at 350°F. for about 10 minutes. Make sure they are cooked thoroughly. If you have any doubts, keep in a heated oven (300°F.) draining on paper towels to finish cooking as well as to keep warm. If the meat must stand awhile, lower oven heat to the lowest point. Do not keep indefinitely in warm oven since the pieces will become dried out.

SAUCE:

2 Tbsp. cornstarch
½ tsp. salt or more
¾ cup sugar
2 tsp. worcestershire sauce
5 dashes tabasco sauce
½ cup vinegar (apple or pine-apple cider type)
½ cup catsup
⅓ tsp. dark molasses or thick soy (optional—use this in-gredient if you wish a dark, deep brown color)
¾ cup juice of pineapple and water combined
2 green peppers, cut in big chunks
2 onions, cut in big chunks
1 large can pineapple chunks, drained (use liquid in sauce)

Blend sauce ingredients. Stir while cooking over medium heat to thicken. Should become quite translucent. Add chunks of vege-tables. Simmer about 2 minutes for vegetables to cook to a rather raw-tender stage. Add pineapple chunks and cook ½ minute more to warm through. Put hot, fried pork cubes into sauce and blend together. Serve over a bed of lettuce shreds.

SUBSTITUTIONS:

Use chicken instead of pork
½ cup carrots, cut ¼ inch diagonally and parboiled 3 minutes
½ cup cauliflower, cut into tiny flowerlets

1 or 2 firm tomatoes, cut in quarters and added at the last minute
1 small bottle of maraschino cherries, drained

Use what you have on hand. Make it attractive and if you wish a brilliant red color, add food coloring. A dash of oil blended in just before you serve the hot sauce will make the surface gleaming, but this is optional.

Buta Nabe—Pork in a Pot (Japanese)

1½ lbs. lean pork, sliced into thin strips ¾ inch by 2 inch by ¼ inch thick
1 tsp. grated ginger
1 large onion, sliced ⅜ inch thick, then cut in half
1 soy bean cake (*tofu*), cut in 1-inch cubes
1 cup or less fresh string beans, sliced diagonally, or carrots, sliced diagonally
1 bunch green onions with tops, 1-inch diagonally sliced

½ cup bamboo shoots, sliced ¼ inch thick
1 cup fresh mushrooms, sliced ¼ inch thick, or dried Japanese mushrooms, soaked in water for 20 minutes, squeezed dry and sliced
Handful of dry bean threads (*sai fun*), soaked in hot water for 15 minutes and cut in 2-inch lengths or use same quantity *shirataki* (yam threads)

SAUCE:

3 Tbsp. sugar
1 Tbsp. sherry, *sake,* or *mirin*
½ tsp. MSG

⅓ cup soy
additional stock or water, if desired

Mix sugar, sherry, MSG, soy and a little stock in a pitcher and have ready for use. Add 1 Tbsp. oil to hot skillet. Add grated ginger and cook pork until white. Sprinkle about half of the sauce mixture over the meat in pan. Bring back to simmering point. Add vegetables and *tofu* (bean cake) carefully arranging the pieces in pan to make an attractive appearance, each in its particular place. Add the remaining sauce mixture. Reduce heat and simmer for 5 to 6 minutes. Add bean threads at the last 1 or 2 minutes of cooking time so that they will not absorb all the juices. The no-color, opaque quality of the bean threads will turn brownish. This is the flavored juices being absorbed into threads. If the threads are too pale looking cook awhile more. Taste. If too bland, add more soy and sugar mixture. Do not overcook.

In Japanese cooking you do not toss-fry. Just turn the vegetables in its specified corner of the pan where they were put in the first place. This retains the visual beauty of the foods even during the cooking process, the greens in one section, the brown meat in another, the orange carrots accenting still a different corner.

Various vegetables could be used. Japanese potato (*taro*), celery, burdock (*gobo*), water chestnuts, peas, spinach, *konyaku* (tuberous root—made into translucent square shape), Chinese cabbage (*nappa*), *bok choy* (Chinese chard), and so on. Chicken can be substituted.

This recipe is similar to *sukiyaki* which cooks at the table (as everyone takes from the central cooking pan) except that this is prepared at the stove and served ready to eat on a serving platter.

Cold servings make a nice picnic lunch with Japanese rice balls. *"Hekka"* (Hawaiian) and *"umani"* are other names for the above with slight variations in seasonings, ingredients and cutting meat, but all more or less the same general family of cooking method.

Chopped Pork With Vegetables (Chinese)

1½ lbs. pork (butt or loin) minced like hamburger meat	2 or 3 ribs celery, diced
1 clove garlic, minced	1 small can bamboo shoots, diced
1 lb. string beans (fresh Kentucky Wonders, diced) or 1 pkg. frozen peas, thawed	1 small can water chestnuts, diced
	1 cup fresh mushrooms, diced
	salt to taste
	iceberg lettuce

GRAVY:

1 Tbsp. sherry	½ tsp. salt
1 Tbsp. *hoisin* sauce	¼ tsp. sugar
1 Tbsp. soy	¾ cup water or stock (more, if
1 to 1½ Tbsp. cornstarch	desired)
½ tsp. MSG	

Heat frying pan over highest heat and add 1 Tbsp. oil. Add garlic and pork. Be sure garlic hits the oil when you put the pork and garlic in pan. Toss-fry until pork is whitish and cooked. Salt to taste. Drain any excess oil. Remove from pan to dish.

Sauté vegetables in frying pan with 1 Tbsp. oil for 1 minute. Keep toss-frying. (For string beans cook ahead of the other vegetables since they will take a few minutes longer to cook. Add a spoonful of water to string beans and allow to steam-fry with cover for about 2 minutes.) Add cooked pork to pan with vegetables. Add gravy ingredients. Stir and cook only until thickened. Keep toss-frying. Shred lettuce thinly and arrange nicely on platter. Pour mixture over lettuce when ready to serve.

Authentically, this is served with lettuce leaves in one bowl and the pork mixture in another bowl. You put a dab of mixture on a lettuce leaf and roll it up like a cigar, or you might compare it with a Mexican *taco*. Hold between fingers and eat!

VARIATION:

Fresh long Chinese string beans, about 1 yard long, are good substitutes for the above Kentucky Wonder string beans.

Nishime—Cooked Vegetables and Meat (Japanese)

This unusual entree is especially suited for New Year's buffet, picnics or whatever. Usually served room temperature. Arrange attractively for serving in stacked lacquered boxes (*jubako*) or on a large platter separating the various ingredients.

1 lb. of cut-up pork or chicken, cut up into 1½ inch by ¼ inch by ¾-inch slices

2 or 3 strips of *nishime konbu* (kelp), 10 inch by 3 or 4 inch wide strips

3 or more dried mushrooms, soaked, washed and squeezed dry. Cut into 1-inch pieces

2 *konyaku,* sliced (tuberous root cakes), sliced ¼ inch thick

3 *aburage* (optional — fried bean cake), run boiling water through them to remove excess oil, cut into pieces

1 large lotus root (*renkon*) or substitute 1 cup *daikon* (radish), cut into chunks

1 cup bamboo shoots, cut into 1-inch chunks

4 *araimo* (*taro*), cut into 1½-inch pieces (both of these are Japanese potato varieties) or substitute 1 or 2 russet potatoes

2 or 3 carrots, cut into 1-inch chunks

1 cup *gobo* (burdock), sliced diagonally into ¼-inch slices and soaked in water until ready for use

1 piece of ginger about 1 inch long, sliced ¼ inch thick

1½ cup water

½ cup soy

⅓ cup sugar

½ tsp. salt

1 tsp. MSG

3 Tbsp. *mirin* (sweet rice wine)

Soak *konbu* and mushrooms in water for about 15 to 20 minutes or longer. Drain. Wash and cut the *konbu* down the center lengthwise, especially, if it is much more than 3 inches wide. Tie into knots 2 inches apart. Cut between knots.

Fry the meat in 1 Tbsp. oil in a deep heavy pot until lightly browned. Add 1½ cup water, mushrooms, *aburage,* ginger and *konbu.* Cover. Cook 10 minutes. Add seasonings and cook for 5 minutes. Add the *renkon* or *daikon,* carrots and *gobo.* Cook another 15 minutes. Remove these vegetables and pork to a serving platter. Reserve remaining liquids and *konbu* for further cooking.

Cook the taro until done, about 15 minutes more in the above liquid along with bamboo and *konyaku.*

VARIATIONS:

Button canned or fresh mushrooms could be used. Fresh string beans could be added for 5 to 7 minutes before cooking in finished. Edible-pod peas could be added 1 minute before serving to maintain crispness. Use your judgment in adding or changing the ingredients. However, do not begin to add watery type vegetables or very strong flavored ones, i.e. cabbage, or you will alter the character of the dish. You could use more chicken and pork, if desired. And there is nothing stopping you from consuming this entree while it is hot!

Lion's Head (Chinese)

This dish is not really made from lion—but the large king-size meat balls imitate the head of the lion and the cabbage is the mane.

1 lb. ground pork	1 tsp. grated ginger
3 dried mushrooms, soaked, squeezed dry and chopped fine (optional)	1 egg, beaten
	1 tsp. sherry
	3 Tbsp. soy (more or less)
6 water chestnuts, chopped fine (optional)	½ tsp. salt
	1 tsp. sugar
½ cup onions, chopped	2 tsp. cornstarch

Mix the above ingredients well. Shape into 3 large balls or more small ones. Fry in 1 Tbsp. oil in hot skillet. Drain excess oil. Arrange 1 head of Chinese *nappa* cabbage, sliced, in a deep pot. Place balls on top. Add 1½ cup hot water. Simmer ½ hour. Serve. With most recipes you simmer much longer and the cabbage gets quite soft and mushy. I prefer more texture so I only cook ½ hour.

You could use only meat—2 lbs. of ground pork and no vegetables mixed into the balls—but the cabbage would be used at the bottom of the pot as above.

Pork With Water Chestnuts Ma Tai Soong (Chinese)

1 large can water chestnuts, minced	1 clove garlic, minced
1 cup lean pork, minced	½ tsp. grated ginger

GRAVY:

½ tsp. salt	¼ tsp. MSG
1 tsp. soy	1 cup plus 2 Tbsp. chicken
1 tsp. sherry	broth (I use a commer-
dash of sugar and black	cially made type)
pepper	1 Tbsp. cornstarch

Heat frying pan on highest heat until hot. Add 1 Tbsp. oil
and when sizzling, add garlic and ginger along with the pork. Be
sure garlic and ginger hit the bottom of the pan. Toss-fry for a
few minutes until pork looks whitish. Drain any excess oil. Add
water chestnuts and the gravy ingredients. Continue to stir-fry
on high heat for 2 or 3 minutes. Cook until sauce is thickened.
Adjust seasonings, if necessary. You may like a bit more soy.
This is rather a bland dish but that is what is appealing about it.
For color, you could add a handful of green peas or edible-pod
peas, although this would not be authentic.

Barbecued Spareribs (Chinese)

4-5 lbs. pork spareribs, uncut	8 Tbsp. catsup
(Chinese use ribs from	½ tsp. saltpeter or substitute 1
small hogs—more tender)	Tbsp. red food coloring
2 cloves garlic, minced	¼ cup sherry
½ cup *hoisin* sauce	dash MSG
⅓ cup soy	2 Tbsp. Chinese parsley,
5 Tbsp. sugar or honey	chopped (optional)

Trim excess fat from ribs. Put in shallow pan and mix ingredients for marinade. Use a pastry brush and paint on both
sides. Marinate for 3 hours at room temperature. Preheat oven
to 375°F. Hang ribs on oven rack (with wires made of large
paper clips, the biggest size available—untwist them to make a
hook). Put a broiler-type large pan filled with hot water just
under the ribs to catch drippings. This will make for moist ribs,
using same method as for the *char siu* (roast pork). Roast about
60 minutes or a bit longer, if ribs are tough. Test to see if done.

You could do this on a *hibachi* charcoal grill. Be sure to cook
long enough or ribs will be tough. Serve hot or cold, cutting each

rib into pieces. Serve with dipping sauces of hot mustard, soy or catsup.

Pork With Dow Fu (Chinese)

¾ to 1 lb. pork, cut in thin slices, ¼ inch by ½ inch by 1½ inches
¾ cup water or stock
3 or more stalks green **onions**, cut in 1-inch lengths
1 *dow fu* (bean cake—Japanese size) cut in flat 1-inch squares ½ inch thick
1 medium size onion, chunks
2 or 3 Tbsp. soy bean condiment (Chinese brown bean paste sold in jars or cans)
grated ginger added with pork

GRAVY:

¼ cup water
1 tsp. cornstarch
1 tsp. soy
dash MSG
1 tsp. sugar
dash salt

Brown pork in hot, oiled frying pan. Mix soy bean condiment and water. Stir and pour into frying pan. Let simmer for 5 minutes. Add onions and bean cake. Pour gravy into frying pan, stirring gently. Let it steam for 1 minute. Add sliced green onions and steam for another minute. Garnish with additional chopped green onions (raw) just before serving.

Various soy bean condiments seem to vary in saltiness so adjust to your desire. You may like more sugar.

Tonkatsu Pork Cutlets (Japanese)

Cut pork tenderloins thick, either as steaks or as bite-size servings. Sprinkle with salt and pepper to taste. Set aside for 5 minutes and then roll meat in flour, slightly beaten egg and then into bread crumbs. Allow to set for 15 minutes or longer so that the crumbs will adhere nicely. Fry the breaded meat in deep-fat, 350°F., turning often. Do not allow to brown too fast since the pork must cook thoroughly. When nicely browned, about 10 minutes (test for doneness), drain on paper towels. Serve with a garnish of finely shredded cabbage (cut like cole slaw) placed on a lettuce leaf cup. *Tonkatsu* sauce can be served with this. It is like a steak sauce and chutney mixed together. Soy or catsup would be acceptable, too.

Chinese Sausage (Lop Cheong) and Bacon (Lop Yuk)

The fresh *lop cheong* (Chinese pork sausage) and *lop yuk* (Chinese bacon) are available in Chinatown, and, also in many other larger cities. They are a marvelous addition to Oriental cookery, and once discovered you will relish the delightful flavor. *Lop cheong* can be used for cooking or for serving as *hors d'oeuvres*. I almost wish I could give you a sample right now! Scrumptious! To prepare, steam for 15 minutes and slice in small pieces, spear with toothpicks and serve with a dip of the usual mustard paste and soy. Or, for an accompaniment with a bowl of hot, steaming rice, it is a meal in itself.

I recommend the fresh pork sausage made in the larger China-towns of the United States as compared to the frozen ones imported from Canada which are quite hard and often have a rancid taste. The fresh product is much nicer in general tenderness and savour, although it is usually more fatty. I feel that, even if the cost is a bit more, it is worth it to purchase superior flavor as opposed to buying something at a somewhat lower cost and of poorer quality.

Whenever I fry *lop yuk* in class demonstrations all the surrounding area becomes so elegantly fragrant with the wonderful aroma that people float by to find out, "What's cooking?" It makes a delicious base for fried rice as well as a substitute for bacon and ham. I do not especially feel it is quite the right flavor for breakfast bacon, but, then I've heard so many things that people eat for morning meals—like cold spaghetti, soup—the sky's the limit. It is all good nutrition, cold *won ton, chow mein*—anything, just be sure to get for breakfast about one-fourth your daily nutritional requirements.

Steamed Chicken and Chinese Sausage

1 chicken fryer about 3 lbs.	½ tsp. grated ginger
5 Chinese sausages (*lop cheong*), steamed 15 minutes first	2 Tbsp. sherry
	½ tsp. salt or more
	½ tsp. sesame oil
4 tsp. water chestnut flour or cornstarch	dash MSG
	2 green onion stalks, chopped
½ tsp. sugar or less	2 Tbsp. Chinese parsley, chopped (this really adds that "special zip")
1½ Tbsp. soy	
1 clove garlic, minced	

Chop chicken, bones and all, in 1 to 2-inch sections. Cut already steamed Chinese sausage, diagonally, into ½-inch slices. Combine water chestnut flour, sherry, salt, sesame oil, ginger and garlic, sugar, soy. Mix well. Add to chicken sections and toss gently to coat. Arrange chicken in a large, deep pyrex dish. Top with Chinese sausages. Steam on a rack until done. Takes about 40 minutes. Garnish with green onions and Chinese parsley. Adjust seasonings, if necessary.

VARIATIONS:

One could coat chicken sections with 4 tsp. of cornstarch and add 6 dried black mushrooms, soaked and squeezed dry, then sliced. Reserve 1 cup mushroom soaking liquid. Add it to the seasonings. Pour this over the chicken, mushrooms and sausages. Steam 40 minutes and garnish as above.

Exotic Sausage—Lop Cheong Soong (Chinese)

4 *lop cheong* (Chinese sausages), diced	½ cup stock
	2 tsp. cornstarch
5 dried mushrooms, minced, after being soaked and squeezed	½ tsp. grated ginger
	½ tsp. sesame oil
	dash MSG
1 small can bamboo shoots, diced	dashes salt and pepper
	1 tsp. rice wine or sherry
½ cup green pepper, diced	dashes of sugar and oyster sauce to taste
2 stalks green onions, minced	
1 small can water chestnuts, diced	½ cup chopped peanuts or almonds, toasted

Sauté *lop cheong* over low flame in frying pan, Remove *lop cheong* from pan. Sauté mushrooms and ginger with sausage fat. Remove mushrooms and ginger from frying pan. Toss-fry bamboo, green pepper, onion and water chestnuts. Return above sautéed ingredients to bamboo shoot mixture and mix. Add cornstarch mixed with stock to thicken gravy. More stock could be added if a more liquid gravy is desired. Add all seasonings to taste. Sprinkle with chopped nuts and Chinese parsley. Serve with lettuce leaves or line platter with shredded lettuce and place the entree on top of the base of greens.

Lop Cheong With Bean Cake

Use 5 thinly-sliced prepared sausages (steam first for 15 minutes until translucent and ready for use) and brown in skillet. Drain most of oil. Add a bean cake (*tofu*) cut into bite-size cubes. Cook with ½ cup stock or water and minced green onions only to heat through. Thicken with cornstarch dissolved in a little water. No further seasonings necessary except for, perhaps, soy and a dash of sugar and MSG. 2 Tbsp. Chinese soy bean condiment adds to good taste with this recipe (optional).

Rice and Chinese Sausages

Lop cheong can be steamed 15 minutes and diagonally sliced (or, you can use without steaming and place directly on rice. This will be more authentic, however, it is more oily). Place atop your Chinese rice as it steams just at the stage when the water has been absorbed into the rice. Continue to steam cook rice at least 25 minutes more. The aromatic flavors marry the rice grains ever so lovingly.

Stir-Fried Lop Yuk and Nappa Cabbage (Chinese)

½ lb. *lop yuk* (Chinese bacon), sliced
1 head *nappa* cabbage
½ tsp. grated ginger
1 Tbsp. oil
1 tsp. salt

¼ cup chicken stock or more
dashes of MSG and sugar
A little cornstarch dissolved in small quantity of water, if thickened sauce desired

Fry *lop yuk* cut into thin slices about 3 minutes. Drain off excess oil. Cut *nappa* cabbage in 1-inch strips. Heat oil in skillet. Add salt and ginger. Stir-fry a few seconds. Add cabbage. Toss-fry 1 minute. Stir in stock and heat quickly. If a bit of thickened sauce is desired, add some of the liquid cornstarch at this point, and stir-fry until vegetables are crisp-tender. Serve with soy.

VARIATIONS:

String beans, edible-pod peas, *bok choy* (Chinese chard), mushrooms or any other vegetable of your choice.

Substitutes for *lop yuk* (Chinese bacon): you can use ½ lb. Chinese sausage, steamed until translucent then chopped or use ½ lb. regular bacon, ham or Canadian bacon.

Fried Rice (Chinese)

½ cup shrimps, shelled, deveined and cut like peas
1 cup cooked chicken, ham or roast pork, cut like peas or substitute *lop yuk*, fried
4 cups cooked rice on dry side. Day-old rice fries better. Or make rice early in the day and keep in the refrigerator. Grains separate nicely this way when cold. Texas patna type is ideal rice for this recipe.
2 eggs, beaten slightly
2 Tbsp, green onions, chopped fine
2 or 3 Tbsp. soy
salt and oil
dash MSG

Heat 2 Tbsp. oil in hot skillet and sauté meat. Scrape to one side and add shrimps and fry until red, adding more oil, if needed. Mix in rice, green onions, soy, eggs, salt, and MSG. Stir until eggs get done.

VARIATIONS:

Use pre-fried bacon or Chinese *lop yuk,* sliced. Drain oil. Serve with more soy or catsup or whatever you like! Add ½ cup onions, celery, green peppers, mushrooms or any other dry-type vegetables. Do not use so much that meat flavors are subdued, just a touch. Use whatever meat you have on hand. If leftover Japanese-style rice is used—it will be a bit gummier although quite tasty. Can be served Oriental fashion by pressing rice into bowl and inverting into another larger bowl.

EGG DISHES

The Orientals make excellent use of eggs in all kinds of dishes. Many of these dishes can be adapted to our American-style menus very beneficially.

Japanese Egg Roll With Spinach

1 egg	cleaned and the pink part
salt	of root left intact
1 small bunch fresh spinach,	soy

Boil spinach quickly in salted water about 3 minutes—just until wilted and bright green in color. Drain and run cold water through it to stop the cooking action. Do not overcook. Squeeze well to remove excess water.

Lightly beat egg with chopsticks to blend. Season with salt. Heat a very little oil in skillet. Remove excess oil with paper towel. Pour egg evenly in hot pan. Turn heat to low and cook until a firm, thin omelet sheet is formed. Try not to brown the bottom. A small rectangular Japanese omelet pan would be ideal for preparing this dish.

Place omelet on bread board. Place spinach in a neat line along the center of the omelet and roll like a jelly roll. Cut into slices crosswise about 1½ inches long. Arrange on platter with open end up. Sprinkle a bit of soy or soy and a dash of sugar and MSG mixed together—let it seep through the spinach. Garnish tops with toasted black sesame seeds, if desired. Serve room temperature. The appearance of the spinach wrapped in yellow egg is most refreshing and would be a delight to serve at any time.

Marbleized Tea Eggs (Chinese)

9 eggs	1 Tbsp. salt
2 tea bags (oolong)	1 star anise (optional)
2 Tbsp. soy	

At least 2 hours before serving hard cooked eggs, simmer eggs for about 15 minutes. Then place under running cold water to cool shell. Roll each egg ever so gently on table to crack the entire shell. But, do not remove the shells. This cracking allows the color to marbleize the egg whites in picturesque etchings.

In a large pan place cracked eggs and add just enough water to cover. Bring up to a boil. Add the tea bags, soy, salt and 1 star anise. Bring back to boiling again and simmer eggs about 5 minutes, uncovered. Discard the tea bags and continue to simmer the eggs, covered, over very low heat for 45 minutes. Turn off heat; leave eggs in this colored, flavored liquid for 1 hour. Serve whole or cut them in half lengthwise, but do not shell until just before serving. Could be served either hot or cold.

Can be eaten for breakfast, between meals or much as we serve stuffed eggs. Placed on the edge of a platter serving some cold cuts, it is most attractive. Or stack them high in a lovely porcelain container, bring them to your next outdoor picnic or put them in your brown bag lunch!

Steamed Custard—A Hot Main Dish (Japanese and Chinese)

We have a tendency to have mental blocks about many of our common foods. We feel custards are for desserts, sweet and served cold. Not so for the Orientals—they have similar methods of preparing this most unusual egg custard. One could almost call it a custard soup. This dish is served hot.

Steamed Egg Custard—Chawan Mushi (Japanese)

4 eggs	1 tsp. MSG
2 cups basic soup stock, i.e. chicken broth or Japanese *dashi* (soup base)	½ raw chicken breast slices of fish cake (*kamaboko*), slices of bamboo shoots, edible-pod peas, fresh watercress or a sprig of edible garland chrysanthemum leaves (*shungiku*)
1 tsp. salt	
1 tsp. soy	
1 Tbsp. *mirin* (Japanese sweet rice wine) or sherry (if sherry is used add 1 tsp. sugar)	

Marinate chicken, cut in thin slices, as well as the vegetables in a little soy. Meanwhile, beat the eggs slightly with chopsticks. Add the soup stock and salt, soy, MSG, *mirin* or the sherry-sugar combination. Pour into individual cups or bowls or leave in one large, heavy pyrex or ceramic type bowl. Place the chicken, fish cake, bamboo, peas and the greens in a small quantity in each bowl or the entire quantity of meat and vegetables in one large bowl. Steam for about 15 to 20 minutes for the small cups, a little longer for the big bowl. Do not have the heat too high or the egg mixture will separate. Test with a knife to see if it comes out clean when withdrawn. Garnish with a thin strip of lemon and parsley. Serve hot.

Chinese Clam Custard—Not a Dessert!

4 eggs	2 cups liquid such as 1 cup minced clams and juice plus 1 cup water
1 Tbsp. oil	
salt to taste	

(One flat can of clams is about 1 cup, so just use your can to measure the water.) Combine eggs with chopsticks in heavy pyrex bowl. Do not use stainless steel bowl as it does not give good results in this special case. The heat retention seems poor. Use salt sparingly since clams have a salty taste already. Add oil. Mix together with clams and liquid. Steam gently about 20 to 25 minutes. Be sure to put a cover on top of the steamer so that the vigorous steam action will be retained. Test with knife to see if center is done, blade should be clean when withdrawn. Sprinkle surface with slivered green onions and 1 Tbsp. soy just before serving. Serve hot.

VARIATIONS:

Use ham, roast pork slices, shrimps, crab, scallops, chicken (cooked or raw). Use chicken broth as the liquid when using these meats for better flavor.

Rolled Omelet—Omoretsu (Japanese)

Omelet is like a miniature jelly roll served cold but with egg flavor!

6 eggs	½ tsp. salt
1 Tbsp. sugar (more or less)	1 Tbsp. *mirin* (sweet rice wine)
6 Tbsp. *dashi* (Japanese soup base or water)	or sherry
	dash of MSG

Mix all ingredients together. Heat rectangular frying pan and oil very lightly. A square pan will work just as well. Pour one quarter of the mixture into the hot pan and cook over medium low heat until the egg is firm but not dry. Starting closest to the handle of the skillet, roll the egg away from you like a jelly roll. Then, slide it back all toward yourself. Leave this rolled egg omelet in the pan. Oil the pan ever so lightly again and pour another quarter of the mixture into the pan. When it is set, roll the first onto the new sheet and continue this jelly roll process to the far end of the pan and push it back near yourself. Repeat until all the egg mixture is used up. Each layer of egg should be partially cooked and rather soft in the center so the layers will adhere to each other. Cool in pan to set the shape better, it will look like an oblong from the edge.

Turn onto a board and cut into 1-inch thick slices. This is a nice addition to a picnic lunch—Japanese fashion. A few par-boiled peas could be sprinkled onto the cooking egg sheets for a variation in color. Do not use too much. Toasted *nori* seaweed could be placed on top of omelet as you roll and a pretty design will be formed when sliced as well as adding to the flavor.

Raw Eggs (Japanese)

A raw egg with soy blended with chopsticks in a small bowl and then, poured over hot, Japanese-style rice makes a delicious snack. A very simple dish and you cannot believe the taste until you have tried it. The raw egg is utilized in Japanese cookery often and once you get used to the flavor, it grows on you. It gets slightly coddled by the hot rice grains. Raw eggs are used as a dipping sauce with some Japanese specialties. With hot *sukiyaki* it is most authentic to dip your food pieces into a sauce dish with raw egg in it, but of course it is good even minus the egg.

Egg Foo Young (Chinese)

1 cup raw shrimps, shelled, deveined and cut into small pea-size pieces or substitute 1 can shrimp or crab, drained
½ cup onion, thin rings, cut in half
½ lb. bean sprouts, washed
½ cup Oriental dried mushrooms, soaked in water, squeezed and sliced thin
½ cup celery, slashed into several thin layers and then cut into matchstick pieces
½ tsp. grated ginger
1 tsp. salt
dash of MSG
1 Tbsp. soy
¼ tsp. sugar
8 eggs, slightly beaten

Mix all ingredients in large bowl. Stir to blend. Use 2 Tbsp. oil in hot skillet and make small pancake patties. Carefully dip a tea cup into the egg mixture and form your patties in pan, making sure that some of the egg drips onto the top surface. When partially set, flip over. Brown both sides.

SAUCE:

2 tsp. soy
2 tsp. cornstarch
½ tsp. sugar
  dash of MSG

salt to taste
½ cup water or chicken stock
  or juices from drained
  shrimp (canned)

Cook until thickened, stirring all the time. Pour over the patties that have been placed on hot platter. Garnish with chopped green onions. If restaurant style is desired, then fry patties in deep-fat being careful to retain shape. Drain on paper towels. Serve with sauce.

CLASSIC JAPANESE DISHES

TEMPURA—A WONDERFUL PARTY IDEA
(JAPANESE)

An informal kitchen party is an excellent idea with *tempura* because there is such a harmony between the chief host and the guests. It is a fun time with everyone around the stove—some asking for shrimp, some for a slice of tender yam and so on.

Tempura cooks have favorite oil combinations but here in America we can rely on a well-standardized name brand for reliability. We do not have to become quite a perfectionist. I feel there is no need for all this fancy work. Select which is your favorite brand after doing several trials. I favor certain ones and you will, too. There is only one caution; I never use a solid type shortening for frying because I feel if it is firm in its cold state it must be like that on the cold, fried pieces. I always use liquid vegetable oils. I use sesame oil sparingly, like a vanilla extract for flavoring a cake, never for frying. Occasionally, you will see a recipe with sesame oil for deep-fat frying. I dislike sesame oil for this purpose since it is quite heavy and too strong in flavor.

The hot oil should be about 350°F. If the oil is too hot, the batter covered fritter will come right up to the top instantly and brown too fast. If too low in temperature, the fried item will remain at the bottom and the *tempura* will be oil soaked. To be just right, the *tempura* should be in the center area of the oil level and gradually float to the top. It should not get deep brown. For *tempura* you want a light golden shade.

I love to utilize the Chinese *wok* for *tempura*. It far surpasses a Japanese shallow *tempura* pan and barely any oil is spilled onto the stove and also less oil is needed because of the conical shape of the pan. We homemakers can appreciate this since we have to do the clean-up chores usually.

A large Chinese 6-inch diameter brass wire skimmer to remove the *tempura* from the deep-fat is fantastic since you can remove a large quantity while it drains at the same time. Skim off any crumbs or dark bits of batter with a slotted spoon or, best of all, use a Japanese net skimmer made expressely for this purpose. It is a fine wire mesh and about 4 inches in diameter.

Serve *tempura* as hot as possible, directly from the hot oil, draining on paper napkins. You want a thin, Japanese-style crisp batter—not a fat, heavy brown pancake wrapped around each morsel of shrimp or vegetable. We would just get filled with dough and even our insides would have pancakes wrapped around them! The amount of batter in the following recipe is sufficient for about 4 to 6 servings. There is a gastronomic delight in seeing the individual fresh ingredients glow through the veil of crispy, thin batter—the delicate pink of the shrimp, the vivid green of the peppers and the string beans as well as the rosy orange of the carrots and the dash of yellow of the yam.

Tempura set on a paper napkin which in turn is placed on a bamboo woven dish, would be exquisite but a lovely plate would be just as nice. Decorate with leaves or flowers in Oriental fashion.

Then, to eat, dip crisp *tempura* into the light exquisite sauce with a condiment or two added, if desired—not a bit oily!

Tempura

Wash and shell about 1 lb. shrimp, leaving on tails. Cut along back, devein, but keep the slash from going all the way through the body. Flatten out the center of the back (butterfly or sometimes called fantail). Slit shrimp in 2 or 3 places to prevent curling. You can soak in ice cubes at this point to chill. Be sure to use paper towels to dry off all ingredients prior to dipping in batter.

Prepare your vegetables: Carrots and string beans cut into julienne strips, sweet potato cut in thin slices (test when frying to see if done), eggplant cut into thin slices, edible chrysanthemum leaves, asparagus sliced diagonally, onions rings separated, fresh mushrooms sliced ¼ inch thick, and so on. You can freely substitute with vegetables that you have on hand such as green peppers, summer squashes, watercress, parsley, edible-pod peas or even try sliced lotus roots.

BATTER:

½ cup flour	1½ tsp. baking powder
½ cup cornstarch	1 egg
½ tsp. salt	1 cup ice water
1 tsp. MSG	

Beat egg and add water. Mix together. Set aside. Mix dry ingredients and add egg mixture to form thin batter. Do not over-mix and make it just before starting the *tempura* frying. Lumps in the batter are all right. Dip shrimp and vegetables one by one, dripping any excess batter at the edge of the bowl. The julienne strips of carrots and string beans could be put into a small bowl and a portion of the batter could be mixed with the strips. Take a spoonful on the edge of the rice paddle and scrape off into the hot oil. A very easy way to slip the thin shreds into the oil. The orange and green combination always looks attractive. If the shrimp or vegetables are still wet, dip first into dry ingredients and then into the batter. Fry very quickly until golden. Drain on towels.

Dip into *tempura* sauce before eating to be authentic. This cuts some of the oiliness of the fritter. *Tempura* can be served with soy alone and perhaps with some *daikon* radish, grated. Gives *tempura* a nice spicy tang. There are all kinds of quick "ready-to-mix" broth type bases at the stores that are excellent for *tempura* sauce. You can make one as follows, if desired.

TEMPURA SAUCE:

3 cups broth such as *dashi* (Japanese soup base) or commercial beef broth	2 Tbsp. soy 1 Tbsp. sugar 1 tsp. MSG

Heat and serve in little sauce dishes near the bowls of rice.

OPTIONAL BATTER 1:

¼ cup dry biscuit mix	7 Tbsp. ice water
¼ cup cornstarch	

Be sure ingredients are dry before deep-frying with this runny batter. Lumps all right.

OPTIONAL BATTER 2:

A 12 oz. package *tempura* batter mix can be used. Blend 1¾ cups ice water and 1 medium size egg, just enough to dampen the dry ingredients. Eggs vary in sizes so leave out about ½ cup of the batter dry mix in case your batter is too thin; you can remedy it by adding this reserved dry mix. Lumps are all right in this batter. These ready-mixed batters are quite improved now and are excellent choices to use, although for economy try using the one made from scratch in the above original recipe.

Warning: With all these *tempura* batters, do not overmix! Just stir enough with chopsticks to blend. Lumps of dry ingredients are desirable. It's a good idea to keep bowl sitting in larger bowl of ice cubes to keep batter icy-cold.

SUSHI—VINEGARED RICE (JAPANESE)

This is really different food and nowhere in the world in any other cuisine is there a similar dish. If one wishes to use the Japanese honorific term, and ladies should especially, you would say *"o-sushi."* The "o" sound is put before certain nouns to denote politeness. However, it is a very difficult term to put just any old place. You can't say *"o-tempura"*—it is incorrect. So, use with discretion and know what you are saying or there may be faint snickers in the background.

As I teach more and more I find the students have no mental blocks like we Orientals toward certain Oriental foods. People tell me after tasting *sushi*—"Why, this could be a rice salad!" And truly it is kind of a salad—vinegar, sugar, MSG, salt and the assorted vegetables and meat or fish—there are more similarities than we might imagine. But, to say "salad" to a *sushi* gourmet would be sacrilegious. This is the wonder of international foods. It is an open gate to gastronomical pleasures!

There are good and mediocre *sushi* makers. Some like it

sweet, some more vinegary and others like it very bland and almost without sharp seasonings. Some have special rules that they follow diligently—always cooking certain ingredients in a very special way—fanning the hot rice carefully, toasting the *nori* seaweed on only one side and countless other ideas.

But for most of us in this busy jet age to do many time consuming chores is not for us. So there are certain short-cuts I have devised to be fast and deliver with skill as close to the authentic product as possible in our homes.

I shall not present the finer details of *sushi*-making. There are as many schools of thought on this as there are ways to make fillings for sandwiches—and this is the "sandwich" of Japan! My way may not be completely authentic but it works without spending hours at it.

Sushi

This is the basic vinegared rice for *sushi.* Prepare 3 cups Japanese-style rice with 3 cups water. Arkansas Blue Rose is my preferred type of rice for *sushi,* however, any other Japanese type will work. Do not use Texas patna long grain rice. It will be most unsatisfactory.

While the rice is cooking, make a vinegar solution by heating the following together and have ready to pour over hot steamed rice.

4 Tbsp. rice wine vinegar	2 tsp. salt
3 Tbsp. sugar	1 tsp. MSG

Increase measurements, as follows, if more flavoring is desired:

6 Tbsp. rice wine vinegar	2 tsp. salt
4½ Tbsp. sugar	1 tsp. MSG

(*Note:* I find for beginners the first recipe is more delicate and to their taste.) When rice is cooked, use a wet rice paddle and put rice into a large mixing bowl. Add vinegar solution to hot rice, carefully fold into the rice without mashing the kernels. Do this very swiftly. Fan to cool. (Some people use electric fans.) This brings out the luster in the rice. Mix lightly from bottom up with wet paddle.

This rice mixed with sauce can be used in making certain *sushi* without further flavorings added, such as *nigiri-zushi*. It can also be used as a base for *chirashi-zushi* and so on with the addition of meat and vegetable combinations. In saying *sushi* when combined with a descriptive adjective, the "s" becomes a "z" phonetically, and sounds like *zushi*.

Aburage

Fried bean curd cake—either rectangular or triangular to use for *inari-zushi* or for chopping up and adding to *chirashi-zushi*.

Aburage (this is pronounced "age" with a short *e* and not like the age denoting the number of years we are). Cut six *age* crosswise in half, carefully, break center portion and make pocket. Place in colander. Run boiling water over *age* until a lot of the oiliness is washed away. Put in large pan and add lots of water. Boil again, if necessary. Wring out water carefully. Drain.

¾ cup chicken stock	2 Tbsp. soy
½ cup raw chicken meat, chopped, or ½ cup raw pork, chopped	1 tsp. sherry or *mirin* (Japanese sweet rice wine)
2 Tbsp. sugar	½ tsp. MSG

Simmer ingredients 5 minutes to cook raw meat, then put "de-greased" *age* in pan with above prepared stock. Place a small saucer on top of *age* so the juices will be absorbed by the *age* as it remains in stock. Turn over the *age* after about 5 minutes of cooking time. Cook all together about 10 minutes in this flavored stock. Watch carefully so pan will not burn. Remove *age*. Drain off juice. Keep flat and press out excess juice. Cool on plate. Tears easily so handle the *age* with care. Save *age* for *inari-zushi*.

Add 1 can (7½ oz.) of *gomoku-no-moto* (prepared vegetables for *sushi*) to the remaining juice and meat from cooking the *age*. Add ¼ cup thawed frozen peas for color. Heat through,

Add the prepared vegetables and meat mixture to the vinegared rice, leaving some of the juice out if too much. Mix carefully from bottom to top using a wet rice paddle. This rice mixture with vegetables and meat can be served on a large platter or in individual bowls and it would be called *chirashi-zushi*. Garnish with thin strips of egg omelet, toasted *nori* seaweed, cut in thin strips, or *beni-shoga* (pickled red ginger), cut in thin strips.

- *Inari-zushi* (cooked *age* filled with flavored rice). The vegetables and meat combination with vinegared rice becomes the filling. Fill the *age* carefully. This much-flavored rice will make filling for about 10 whole *age* cut in half if filled lightly (20 filled *inari-zushi*). Or make 6 whole *age* and serve balance as loose *sushi*. Please do not pack in the rice. Place the filled *age* with the opening side down and allow to "set" awhile to hold a good firm shape. I have heard this prepared *age* called rice or gunny sacks, footballs and rice bags by non-conventionalists in America. Maybe you'll develop a favorite name yourself.
- At home, my family has always termed them "footballs" and when people would hear us discussing that footballs were on the menu for dinner, they would look at us with very inquisitive stares!
- The vinegared rice alone can be mixed with toasted black sesame seeds and used as a filling for the prepared *age*.
- The prepared *age* could be chopped up and added with the vegetables and the meat to the vinegared rice.
- If you desire to prepare this vegetables and meat combination without the *age,* reduce the stock to ⅓ cup and proceed to simmer meat 10 minutes. Add the *gomoku-no-moto* (canned prepared vegetables for *sushi*). Add peas, if desired, for color. Heat through. Add to vinegared rice, draining off extra juices if there is too much liquid.

These *sushi* variations make excellent picnic fare. It is at its best when made the same day it is to be consumed and not refrigerated, except in dire emergency. It is highly perishable (the reaction of the acid on the starches) so keep in a cool place covered with foil. The rice kernels will get hard if kept in the refrigerator, but if there is any left, by all means put it in the refrigerator. Cover well with foil.

This "toned down" recipe for *sushi* is very mild in flavor. Some people like it much stronger. Experiment until you get the taste that is most agreeable to you. Accurate flavor test is done when the *sushi* is cold and the seasoning has had a chance to penetrate throughout. The *sushi* and its many variations are served at room temperature, not hot or icy-cold.

MORE IDEAS ABOUT SUSHI:

Bits of cerise red *beni-shoga* (pickled ginger) go well with *sushi*. The salty, pungent flavor just hits the spot. Cut match stick, slivered pieces for garnish to really be eaten, not just looked at, when the *sushi* is served.

Often, a garnish of shrimps called *oboro* is used. To prepare, use a 5 oz. can of shrimps. Wash, drain and mash shrimps. Place in small frying pan. Add a few drops of red food coloring to 2 tsp. sugar and mix with shrimp. Add 1 tsp. MSG and cook. Stir over low heat until the shrimp is flaky and dry.

By using various wooden and plastic molds, one can make quite a variety of *sushi,* each with a favorite topping, such as parboiled shrimp and a layer of Japanese horseradish; bits of egg omelet combined with crumbled *oboro* (red-colored shrimp flakes, see recipe above) or raw fish.

Seaweed wound rolls of vinegared rice are called *nori-maki* or *maki-zushi*. They have strips of assorted flavored fillings. The rolls must always have a certain odd number of strips, never an even number, according to the traditionalists. It does get complicated. I wouldn't worry about it, just put in whatever you like. I have eaten a very "all-American" *maki-zushi* with a strip of baloney in it! These cylinders of seaweed and rice are made by rolling with the aid of a bamboo mat called a *sudare*. Egg omelet can, also, be used for the outside covering along with kelp (prepared variously with seasonings) as a different tasting roll. These are sliced into ¾-inch slices and arranged beautifully on lovely decorative platters for serving. Exquisite garnishes are elaborately made for these displays of rice "sandwiches."

Nigiri-Zushi

Place a piece of vinegared fish and a dab of *wasabi* (horse-radish) on a damp cheesecloth or cloth napkin, fish side down. Put 2 Tbsp. vinegared rice (refer to recipe at beginning of this *sushi* section) on top of the fish and *wasabi*. Bring the napkin to a tight closure and form a good, tight ball of the rice and fish inside. Release the cloth easily onto a plate, turning the *sushi* upright with the fish on top. Proceed with your next decorated creation. These make bite size *sushi*. Other toppings could be shrimp, squid and so on. These can also be made by forming with dampened hands. These are specialty foods and so many excellent books are now available that I ask you to seek more information from these sources.

VINEGARED FISH SLICES FOR NIGIRI-ZUSHI:

Sprinkle lightly salt and MSG on cleaned, small raw fish fillet slices (like *sashimi*). Marinate at room temperature for 2 hours.

Dip in the following:

1½ Tbsp. rice wine vinegar	3 Tbsp. cold water
1 tsp. sugar	dash MSG

Drain and follow directions above for *nigiri-zushi* with raw fish. One could use egg omelet as well as the seafoods for the topping, if desired.

O-MIZUTAKI (JAPANESE)

Guest-participation dinners are decidedly friendship builders and this is a true friendship dish—it warms the insides against the outside wind and rain, especially during the winter seasons. There is a coziness about cooking together over one common pot. The *o-mizutaki*—water cooking Japanese-style, or its companion Chinese or Korean methods, all use a hot pot—it has a chimney-like spout, built in like an angel food cake pan, burning charcoal. We can substitute our electric skillets very adequately.

Your whole makeup can warm to give forth a very spirited cheer when sharing together and you will certainly be the best of friends when you finish your Oriental "fondue." Remember that this Oriental-style *"o-mizutaki"* is the fruit of any chef's kitchen, sink and cupboard. You get whatever is handy and put it all together in a beautiful arrangement. You can have a party quite simply or elaborately as you choose. This is one of my favorite ways to cook. You actually only prepare the ingredients —the guests cook for themselves. Go through the refrigerator and select all the potential ingredients and everything will go very swiftly.

When you have "first-timers" at this sort of cooking get-together, they will learn how very short the cooking time for Oriental food ingredients is. Certain common vegetables that you may have been practically destroying by cooking 20 to 25 minutes you will now find they can cook in only 2 or 3 minutes. You will revel in these new taste sensations! What you hated before will now become your favorite vegetables, cooked Oriental fashion, so delicious and digestible, greaseless, too.

You can substitute freely in this recipe. The Japanese actually use a fish and seaweed soup base *(dashi)* but I prefer the American-style commercial broth.

O-Mizutaki or Shabu-Shabu Nabe (Japanese)

2 lbs. beef (such as flank, *sukiyaki* meat, rib eye, top sirloin beef) thinly sliced. If slices are too awkward roll up cigarette-shape

½ head Chinese cabbage (*nappa*), sliced in 1-inch widths

1 bean cake (*tofu*), cut in 1-inch pieces

1 onion, halved and sliced in ½-inch slices

½ lb. fresh mushrooms, sliced ½ inch thick

1 large can bamboo shoots, sliced diagonally

1 green pepper (optional), sliced in ¾-inch strips

1 or 2 carrots, ¼ inch, sliced diagonally

2 ribs celery, ¼ inch, sliced diagonally

a dash of salt and sherry added to broth as well as dash of MSG

beef broth or chicken broth

Fill skillet ⅔ full with equal parts of very slightly seasoned beef broth (commercial or homemade type) and water. Bring to boil, place your sliced beef into boiling soup first. Cook until rareness is just gone. Remove from broth. Continue cooking vegetables in the same manner, little by little. Do not let go of the portion that you submerge in broth or it will become overcooked.

Everyone does his own cooking either with chopsticks or with miniature brass wire spoons (Chinese). As the food cooks you eat it piping hot, dipping in your sauce dish of condiments and sauce. The following is a very light type sauce and extremely popular.

½ cup lemon juice ½ cup soy
dash of MSG

Combine the soy, lemon juice and MSG. Add to it any of the condiments to make your special dipping flavors. Most of us put a little of everything in it. Use several fondue plates for serving condiments, it simplifies having a small dish for this or that. It is easier on the diners, too, not to have the constant "please pass the sesame seeds, the seaweed, please, please and so on." One does not have to use all of these—they are suggestions.

grated fresh ginger
grated *daikon* (radish)
chopped green onions
Japanese red pepper *(togarashi)*
toasted *nori* seaweed
toasted sesame seeds, slightly crushed
lemon wedges
wasabi paste (horseradish)
sansho (Szechwan pepper—fresh is ideal; otherwise, dried crushed powder)

Even to add a pinch of each of the above to your sauce is quite delightful and a definite spark for the *o-mizutaki*.

Shabu-shabu nabe translated means the actual swishing sound of beef and vegetables through the bubbling broth in the pan (*nabe*). Let guests swish their own. After all the ingredients have been consumed, make a soup by adding bits of all the condiments and flavor with the sauce. If broth becomes evaporated and too concentrated, add more water during cooking process. Drink this broth with rice or noodles at the end of the meal, it is scrumptious since it is filled with so many wholesome, flavor-teasing combinations. It is almost like ambrosia!

The Chinese and Koreans, as well as many other nationalities, have similar "cook-it-yourself" meals. There are the fondues— some use broth, some cheese, some chocolate, some oil, or anything and everything that you want, really. It is a very inventive type of cookery.

Sukiyaki (Japanese)

This is pronounced *ski'yaki* but, whatever way you say it, you should have no trouble being understood. *Sukiyaki* is prepared in a more or less continuous process at the table. As soon as the first batch is ready, then the next is started. In the meanwhile, small portions of the hot cooked foods are being consumed. Authentically, the hot pieces are dipped in beaten raw egg and devoured with bowls of hot steamed rice (Japanese-style rice, please). The raw egg bit could be omitted if you do not go for the idea. But at least try it sometime, you may discover you like it. I do.

1½ to 2 lbs. *sukiyaki* meat available at Oriental stores or slice thin about ⅛ inch by 1 inch by 2 inches— top sirloin, fillet, Spencer steaks, or rib eye beef

1 cup fresh mushrooms or dried Oriental ones, soaked in water, squeezed and sliced

2 or 3 pieces of beef suet to grease pan and discard

1 bulb onion, halved and cut in ½-inch slices

2 bunches green onions, cut diagonally in 1½-inch lengths

6 oz. can of *shirataki* (yam noodles) or small handful of bean threads, soaked in hot water for 15 minutes and cut into 2-inch lengths

1 cup bamboo shoots, sliced

½ lb. fresh spinach, cut 2 inches long

1 or 2 ribs of celery, sliced diagonally

½ or 1 block of bean cake (*tofu*), cubed (optional)

raw eggs for dipping (optional)

SAUCE:

½ cup soy   ¾ tsp. MSG
 4 Tbsp. sugar   ¼ cup sherry or *mirin*
½ cup beef broth or *dashi* or
    water

Heat electric skillet at the table, oil it thoroughly with suet. Remove suet. Then place about one-third of the meat slices in pan, one by one, so as not to lay one slice on top of another. Cook until meat juices start oozing out. Then turn over meat. Sprinkle with some of the sugar, soy, broth, MSG and sherry mixture to suit your taste. Do not use all of this broth combination at this time, but reserve part of it to add later as the next batches are being added.

When the meat is partially cooked, put the meat in one corner of the pan. Add a quarter of the vegetables to skillet. Keep each individual vegetable in its special place. Add more broth combination, if desired. Cook very briefly. If necessary to turn over vegetables, do so in its special place in the pan. Remember that this is Japanese cooking and we do not do toss-frying methods with *sukiyaki*. Maintain a good aesthetic appearance. Taste and add more soy or sugar if you desire. Cook only about 3 minutes to 5 minutes. Should be most crispy and yet not raw. Dip cooked meat and vegetables into beaten egg and eat with hot bowl of Japanese-style rice. Before skillet becomes empty add more ingredients and sauce combination. Keep successive servings cooking. *Sukiyaki* is tastiest when eaten piping hot directly from the pan.

VARIATIONS:

Use chicken or pork and cook proportionately longer. Other vegetables that could be used are string beans, carrots, bean sprouts, *nappa* cabbage, green peppers, or whatever you like. Be sure to keep proportions of meat and vegetables correct or *sukiyaki* will not have the proper flavorings.

SEAFOOD DISHES

The charm of the Oriental methods of preparing seafood is what makes fish and shellfish so brilliant-tasting. They often combine vegetables to increase the "protein" portion and the excellence of the dish becomes even better because of the harmony of many ingredients. Fresh ginger is used to cancel the "fishiness" of many dishes so that we odor-conscious Americans can in a very subtle way deodorize our kitchens!

Many feel that fish is the main diet ingredient for the Japanese. They do consume far more fish than we do—but certainly in the modern Japan of today, the availability of many varied food ingredients has altered the Japanese diet, much as it has ours in America. In large, modern cities of Japan, there are some of the most fantastic international restaurants in the world.

Fresh fish is the ideal and best for all cookery but for some of us to get good, fresh fish is a very difficult task. If we are lucky enough to live near the wharf or a good fish store it is simple, but most of us are not that fortunate. Certainly, it does not add to our gastronomical pleasure if we have to work so hard to find fish. It would make eating fish too complicated and erratic.

One can always use fresh salmon, seabass and so on, but when it comes to some of the unfamiliar fish names we get stumped. Therefore, I have experimented with fish that is easily available in the supermarkets and most fish stores, so that you would not have to go catch your own!

Here is my choice—*mahi-mahi* (dolphin), not the dolphins we think about doing tricks at the marine-lands. This is a fish (*Coryphaena hippurus*). Some of you who have been to Hawaii or the Baja, Mexico area have no doubt eaten this delicious fish fresh. The texture is somewhat like swordfish. This is available in Western markets as a frozen product. It keeps very nicely in the freezer for months without any flavor loss. It is relatively inexpensive since there is no waste. And it is there in your freezer when you crave fish! *Mahi-mahi* has a distinct, slightly sweet flavor. I am sure that you will be enthusiastic with this taste discovery.

Fish Teriyaki (Japanese)

2 lbs. fish slices (*mahi-mahi* or whatever you like)	dash MSG
	4 Tbsp. soy
1 tsp. grated ginger	2 Tbsp. sherry or *mirin*
1 clove garlic, minced	2 Tbsp. sugar
½ of an onion, minced	1 tsp. dry mustard

Marinate all together in a bowl for 1 or 2 hours. Broil on rack in broiler or on charcoal *hibachi*. Do not overcook. If moderate-size pieces, they could be done in 5 minutes or a bit more on each side. Serve hot with grated *daikon,* long, white Japanese radish, and soy.

Slightly fat fish is better for *teriyaki* than lean types. Suggestions might be salmon, sea bass, striped bass and yellow tail.

Shio-Yaki—Salted Broiled Fish (Japanese)

The simplest and one of the most exciting of Japanese fare is *shio-yaki.* The natural flavors of the fish are utilized in this dish. With some hot, steamed rice and some pickled vegetables you have a very satisfying meal. Fresh sardines (where have they gone?), mackerel (*saba*), Spanish mackerel (*aji*), tuna (*maguro*), yellowtail (*buri*) and even anchovies are all exquisite this way.

Get fresh fish, scale, but leave head, skin and tail intact. Slash the surface of the skin with several diagonal cuts. Sprinkle prepared fish with salt. Place fish on greased grill or a well-salted cookie sheet. No sticking! Broil carefully, 15 to 20 minutes, and only until done, do not cook too long. Serve with soy.

Salmon Miso-Yaki (Japanese)

2 lbs. salmon slices	2 Tbsp. sugar
½ lb. white soy bean paste (*shiro-miso*)	dash MSG
	2 Tbsp. *mirin* (sweet rice wine)
2 Tbsp. soy	or sherry

Mix all ingredients except fish and blend well. One can put fish in bowl and marinate completely covered for a day or so and then broil. Or spread marinade over fish slices as if you were spreading peanut butter on bread, then allow to marinate in refrigerator for ½ day. Heat your broiler pan first, then place slices on hot pan, *miso* side up. Broil for 10 minutes, without turning, until fish is cooked through. *Miso* browns easily, so watch carefully and lower broiler heat if necessary.

Steamed Fish (Chinese)

One can use almost any kind of flavorful fresh fish; however I have sought out fish that is readily available, inexpensive and keeps well in the freezer for immediate use when one suddenly desires fish—and we all have those times!

I have discovered one of the nicest, tastiest fish—clean, boneless Greenland turbot fillet or what used to be called halibut fillet. It is delicate in flavor prepared this way and the main advantage is that one can buy this fish frozen and keep it on hand. The flavor is retained exceptionally well over many months. Turbot is exceedingly mild in flavor prepared in this Chinese manner. Of course, salmon, striped bass, red snapper and rock cod, to mention a few, are unsurpassed this way, too. I mention turbot because we are trying in this book to be practical, to improve our family cooking style and at the same time, to enjoy gourmet flavors.

I like to serve this fish dish along with an assortment of other foods when I have a dinner. It is an easy addition to prepare, keeping the steamer going at the back of the stove or even setting up a make-shift one on top of the electric skillet, out on the patio. Almost everyone likes the fish this way, even kids!

Clean thoroughly 2 lbs. sea bass, black bass, shad, white fish, mackerel, red snapper, ling cod or whatever is your fancy. The Greenland turbot fillet is excellent for this recipe.

1 tsp. salt	1 Tbsp. chopped cooked ham or
1 tsp. MSG	bacon (optional)
2 Tbsp. soy	4 Tbsp. ginger, shredded fine
4 Tbsp. oil	(use less, if desired). This
2 green onions, slivered	much ginger seems like a
1 clove garlic, crushed	lot but it truly adds to the
	delicate flavor.

Put fish in pyrex pie plate. Put an elevated rack in a large pot containing 3 inches of boiling water; put plate on rack. Cover and steam for 15 to 20 minutes. Usually, fish is done in this very short period. Do not overcook. Fish is done when it flakes easily with a fork. Drain all liquid from plate; add salt. Sprinkle with MSG and soy over fish. Heat oil in saucepan until smoking; add garlic; turn off heat. Let oil cook garlic for one minute. Discard garlic. Pour hot oil over the fish. It should sizzle! Sprinkle ham, ginger and green onions on top of each serving.

The ideal method for steaming is to use the regular Oriental steamer pans that fit into the *wok,* since there is less chance for the boiling water to get on the plate. Keep the water briskly boiling. Add more boiling water from kettle, if necessary.

You will be happy to know that this method of preparation does not fill the air with "fishy" smells. Pans are also easier to clean. I like this method of fish cookery so much I think I could eat it this way daily. One does not tire of this sort of simple fare.

Dry-Fried Shrimp (Chinese)

2 lbs. shrimps, large size. Do	1 tsp. salt
not shell	2 Tbsp. sherry or as much as ½
1 tsp. grated ginger	cup, if desired
2 stalks green onions, chopped	dash of MSG
1 clove garlic, minced	dash of sugar
1 Tbsp. oil	dash of soy

Wash shrimps. If desired, devein, but leave the shells on. (It is often just as easy to let the diner devein the shrimp after he removes the shell.) Dry on paper towels. Heat skillet dry. Add oil. Add garlic, salt, MSG, sugar and soy. Add shrimps and stir-fry a few minutes. Lower the heat. Cover. Cook for a few minutes. Mix shrimps so all surfaces will be cooked.

Sprinkle some ginger and green onions on top. Cover and cook one more minute. Turn up heat and toss-fry to mix well. Pour in the sherry. Cover to blend flavors but turn off heat. Let stand one more minute. Serve hot or cold. Wonderful for snacks or anytime and goes especially well with drinks.

VARIATION:

Leave out the seasonings above and substitute some *Tokyo-zuke* (Japanese pickles) at the same time you add the green onions. Use the sherry, however, since it does add flavor. Add 2 Tbsp. chicken stock while frying if you wish a bit more moisture to dish.

Upon occasion, I have made this ahead and kept it standing since the company was delayed. It did not seem to hurt the end product. Although, I would not advise it as regular practice, it is nice to know it works. Having shells on the shrimp helps to slow down the intake by your guests since they have to take time to shell them.

Chinese-Style Shrimp Fritters

Chinese fritters have a heavier batter than the Japanese version of fried shrimps. Shell and devein 2 lbs. of shrimp. Keep tails intact. Flatten out (butterfly) or leave whole. Keep icy-cold. Dry with paper towels and dip in batter. Deep-fry quickly in oil about 350°F. Drain on paper towels. Arrange on platter lined with thinly sliced lettuce shreds. Serve with sweet and sour sauce. Garnish with slivered green onions and Chinese parsley.

BATTER:

1½ cup flour
½ cup cornstarch
1 egg yolk, beaten
1½ cup ice water

dash salt
dash MSG
1 egg white, beaten stiffly

Mix the dry ingredients in a bowl. Blend the beaten yolk and ice water in a small bowl. Add to the flour mixture just enough to mix. Do not overblend and lumps are all right. Fold in the stiffly beaten egg white.

SWEET AND SOUR SAUCE:

2 tsp. soy	several drops red food
2 Tbsp. cornstarch	coloring
½ cup sugar	1 cup water or fruit juice, like
6 Tbsp. vinegar	pineapple
5 Tbsp. catsup	dash MSG

Mix sauce ingredients together and cook over medium heat stirring constantly until translucent. Pineapple or lichees can be added to sauce.

Crispy Fried Squid

This odd ocean shellfish, sometimes called "ink fish" because of the black coloring matter that squirts out at time of danger, is unknown by many. The Orientals and Italians have been using this squid in many delectable ways for centuries! Here is an Americanized version that will surprise you—it is tender and delicate in flavor like abalone. From this taste-testing, you may eventually want to try to prepare it as *tempura* or a one-pot dish. It is most inexpensive so do try it. Do not overcook it since there is a tendency for squid to get tough.

1 lb. fresh or thawed frozen	¼ cup flour
squid	¼ cup fine bread crumbs
garlic salt	oil

Clean squid by removing the thin black spotted membrane skin. Pull out the transparent shell bones. Clean out all the internal organs. Be sure that you do not break the tiny ink sac. The ink is harmless, just doesn't glamorize the ivory white skin coloring of the squid. Rinse out the cavity called mantle. Save the tentacles. Pop out the beak from the portion that forms the legs as well as cut off the eyes.

Slice the mantle across into ½-inch-wide strips so they look like miniature circles of onion rings. Drain and dry squid with paper towels. Sprinkle with garlic salt. Coat squid with the mixture of flour and crumbs. Allow to stand 10 to 15 minutes. Deep-fry in oil heated to 375°F. Fry a spoonful at a time till lightly browned—only about ½ minute. Gets tough if overcooked. Fry the rings first and then the tentacles. Drain on towels. Keep warm. Eat plain, with soy, a sweet and sour sauce or even catsup. You will wonder why you waited this long to try squid at its best!

Deep-Fried Squid With Batter

1 lb. fresh squid	½ tsp. salt
½ cup flour	1 egg
¼ cup cornstarch	⅓ cup water
½ tsp. baking powder	1½ Tbsp. oil

Clean squid and cut each in four parts. Pat dry with paper towels. Blend together flour, cornstarch, baking powder and salt. Then slightly beat the egg and blend in along with the water and the oil. Mix batter until smooth. Dip squid in this batter to coat. Deep-fry in hot oil, 350°F. Add squid a few pieces at a time and fry until golden. Serve with soy or make a sweet and sour sauce. Pour over fried squid.

Squid can also be served in a myriad of ways—raw (*sashimi*), or cooked in flavored soy sauce, or stuffed and baked (Italian). But these I will leave up to you to seek.

Raw Fish Sashimi (Japanese)

One can become quite a devotee of raw fish. It is better than steak for many of us, that is, if you have excellent quality fish. It must be absolutely fresh—no fishy tastes, no fishy smells. It is one of the most exquisite dishes of Japanese cuisine, with its delicate and most enchanting, gauzy appearing sheer slices so artistically arranged on a platter—be it small and dainty servings or large and decorative displays. The thinly shredded *daikon* radish, lettuce or *nappa* cabbage, the bits of *sansho* leaves with soy and ginger and perhaps *wasabi* (horseradish) make it most appetizing! *Sashimi* is one of the easiest meals for a hot summer day. This can be made up as an appetizer for cocktails and is a favorite *hors d'oeuvre*.

1 lb. fresh sea bass, boned, or fresh tuna or striped bass, filleted	radish) mixed with a little water
shredded lettuce	wedges of lemon
dry mustard mixed with a little water	1½ tsp. grated fresh ginger soy
wasabi (Japanese horse-	MSG
	grated *daikon* radish

Remove all the skin and dark portions from the boneless fish. The ideal section is the back center fillet. Cut diagonally across the fish into very thin slices. Chill. Arrange fish on shredded lettuce or Chinese *nappa* cut in thin shreds. *Daikon* radish can be crisped in iced water after it has been shredded. Serve with your desired condiments: grated ginger, mustard paste, MSG, soy or *wasabi*. Lemon juice cuts some of the rawness of the fish. Your best bet to assure freshness is to catch your own!

Raw Fish and Poultry

Raw fish is also used atop small mounds of vinegared rice. The favorite being *maguro* (tuna) *sushi* with a bit of *wasabi* (horseradish) between the fish and the rice ball. You can dip the fish portion in soy, if desired, as you eat it. Hold onto the fish or it may just decide to slide off!

Raw chicken meat can also be eaten. Slice chicken meat thin and dip in salted boiling water for about 3 minutes. Then, quickly dip in cold water. Serve with grated ginger or *wasabi,* soy and your favorite shredded raw vegetable.

The Italians eat raw chicken breasts, sliced, marinated in lemon juice. It is quite delicious, too! Very similar dishes are consumed all over the world.

Abalone Sashimi (Japanese)

If you are a skin diver and are fortunate to be near the Pacific Ocean, there are still abalones left to be discovered. They are pried off of the craggy rocks with tire irons in fairly deep waters. There was once a time when they were closer to shore but as people came to California and discovered this delectable mollusk, the supply dwindled. Whole fresh abalones are not impossible to find in the Pacific Coast fish markets. Many come from Mexico. Do not use the store-pounded slices for *sashimi*— they are too tenderized and the flavor has often been washed away.

I like to use 2 wooden rice paddles and insert from the opposite sides of the shell to release the muscle. Scour the meat well with salt to remove the darkened coloring. Trim the hard portions and save for future use as broth. Take the heart—the very white part of the meat—and put it into a large plastic bag. This helps to keep the juices from spattering. Pound the abalone with a wooden mallet gently. Wash well. Cut in half. Slice into thin, even pieces. Place on a bed of shredded lettuce. With a small mound of *wasabi* (horseradish) paste and another similar mound of a grated ginger or *daikon* radish, grated, plus wedges of lemon and a bit of soy—this raw abalone *sashimi* is an epicurean delight! What, raw abalone? Think about the raw oysters or clams that you might have swallowed or eaten. This is not any different! I like this texture better.

Abalone (Canned)

The canned abalone from Mexico are of the best quality. The texture is better and much more dependable as compared with the ones packed in Australia. It may be in the canning process but some brands are finer quality than others. Look for good color rather golden-tan shade, firm texture and certainly, not so rubbery that when you chew it you are forever masticating! You can freeze what you do not use and the result is most satisfactory. No loss of flavor or texture.

It makes wonderful eating right from the can—sliced, cubed or whatever, with toothpicks inserted for *hors d'oeuvres,* with lemon and soy for dip or sliced and served for a dinner entree. No need to cook it as it is already processed and ready for use as it comes from the can. Combine it with salads—Oriental or what have you. Save the broth for a delicious soup.

Canned Abalone Soup

Juice from 1 pound can of abalone (Mexican pack, if available)
water as needed
2 cups chicken or pork stock
green onions, slivered

a few drops of sesame oil
½ tsp. soy
1 Tbsp. sherry
¼ cup slivered slices of abalone
dashes of salt and pepper

Measure the juice from the abalone can and to it add enough water to make 2 cups. Combine this with 2 cups of chicken or pork stock. Add soy and sherry. Heat, correct seasonings and serve. Add abalone at the very last moment. Do not overcook. Garnish with green onions and the sesame oil (which gives a wonderful fragrance). A very thin strip of lemon peel is an additional nice touch. Do not try to make this soup with fresh abalone. It will not work.

Abalone Braised in Oyster Sauce (Chinese)

Half of a large can of abalone, thin ⅛-inch slices
3 to 5 large Oriental dried mush-

rooms, soaked in water and squeezed dry, sliced into ⅛-inch slices

GRAVY:

1 tsp. soy
1½ Tbsp. oyster-flavored sauce
1 tsp. cornstarch dissolved in

3 Tbsp. abalone juice from can
dash sugar
dash MSG

Heat abalone and mushrooms in oiled hot pan. Add gravy ingredients. Toss-fry until thickened, about 2 or 3 minutes. Do not overcook. If a bit more gravy is desired, add a tablespoon or so of water. Garnish with chopped green onions.

Fresh Clams (Easy Japanese-Style)

25 fresh clams
1 egg white, slightly beaten
salt

rice wine (*mirin*) or sherry
MSG
lemon wedges and soy

Wash clams in shells. Put a knife between the shell of the clam. Carefully sever any parts that are holding the shell intact. Paint each clam shell with a pastry brush dipped in egg white. Cover entire surface of shells with a layer of salt.

Place the muscle-cut clams still in shells on a hot griddle. Heat for 7 minutes. Open carefully and add a bit of wine and MSG. Serve with lemon wedges and soy.

ALTERNATE METHOD:

Bake clams at 425°F. oven for 5 to 6 minutes. Carefully lift up the top shell and sprinkle clam meat with rice wine, salt and MSG. Close shells. Be careful not to spill juices when serving.

Arrange 5 clams on each plate. One could garnish with a few pine needles and a lemon wedge for a Japanese look.

Dried Oysters (Chinese)

Dehydration results in a stronger flavor and sometimes a different taste in some respects to the fresh products. For instance, mushrooms, shrimps, oysters, abalone, squid, and so on. So use sparingly.

Soak dried oysters all day in water. Drain and they are ready for use. Do not over-soak or the flavor will be weakened. In a pinch, you can boil in water and hasten the softening process.

Shee Soong—Minced Dried Oysters and Pork With Assorted Vegetables (Chinese)

3 or 4 large oysters, soaked all day in water, chopped fine
1½ cup raw pork, chopped fine
1 cup celery, chopped fine
1 small can water chestnuts, chopped fine
1 cup onions, chopped fine
½ pkg. frozen peas, thawed, or edible-pod peas, chopped (these peas are optional and I add them for color —authentically, they are not used)

1 clove garlic, minced fine
½ tsp. grated fresh ginger
½ to ¾ tsp. sugar (to taste)
1 cup stock or water
1½ Tbsp. soy
½ tsp. MSG
¾ tsp. salt
¼ tsp. sesame oil
1 Tbsp. sherry
1 Tbsp. cornstarch
little bit of thick soy or thick molasses to color (optional)

Heat frying pan sizzling hot. Add oil. Add garlic and ginger. Add meat and lightly brown. Add oysters after you drain the oil from the meat. Add mixture of stock or water, sugar, soy, MSG, salt, sesame oil, sherry, thick soy and cornstarch. Dash of pepper can be added if desired. Simmer about 5 minutes. Add the various chopped vegetables and stir-fry for about 3 minutes. Adjust seasonings, if necessary.

Serve hot with steamed rice—pouring the combination on top of rice. This is sort of a Sloppy Joe. For true Chinese flavor, you can add a few more dried oysters. This will result in a strong fishy taste but it is more flavorful that way.

BLACK SALTED BEANS (CHINESE)

These beans are called *dow see*. Wash in a strainer to remove the excess salt and any sediment present, but do not overdo it. You will wash away part of the goodness of this flavoring. The very penetrating smell of this seasoning material is not from the beans and the salt as the label of the ingredients would lead you to believe. Some pieces of dried fish are there, too, which accounts for the pungent odor. Now, you know why, while shopping on a warm day, the car had that strange smell. Put *dow see* into a jar when you store it, or at least place the container in several plastic bags.

My very ingenious students have devised more ways to use many strange Oriental ingredients. To use these black beans and get all of their goodness and, yet not penetrate the entire house with its pungency—they fry the "phewey" beans in the garage or out on the patio with an electric skillet and let the smell disappear into the atmosphere. When the entire dish is ready, they bring the finished, ever-so-elegant entree, to the table. This *dow see* is the prime ingredient for the following Shrimp in Lobster Sauce recipe.

Shrimp Cantonese or Lobster Sauce With Shrimp (Chinese)

1 lb. raw shrimps, shelled and deveined	black beans, washed and drained
½ cup pork, minced	2 cloves garlic, minced
1 or 2 eggs (whites only or whole eggs)	1 green pepper, cut in chunks
2 or 3 tsp. fermented salted	1 onion, cut in chunks

GRAVY:

1 Tbsp. soy	1 Tbsp. cornstarch
1 Tbsp. sherry	¼ tsp. MSG
½ tsp. salt	¾ cup water or stock
½ tsp. sugar	

Butterfly (cut down almost all the way across when deveining and flatten out) shrimps. Wash and drain. This method makes the shrimp curl ever-so-prettily during the cooking process. Crush washed black beans and minced garlic with the side of your cleaver. I usually try to do it on the corner of the bread board so it won't be such a mess to clean up later. Wash and cut green pepper and onion in big chunks with at least 1-inch sides.

Stir-fry onions and green peppers with 1 Tbsp. oil in hot oiled pan until warmed through. Salt. Remove to dish. Heat 1 Tbsp. oil in pan over highest heat. Add bean and garlic. Stir-fry a few times. Add pork and keep stirring until pork turns white. Add shrimps until cooked—they will turn pinkish. It only takes about 5 minutes to do this. Add gravy ingredients, mix well. Keep your toss-frying action going and cook for about 3 minutes to thicken the gravy. Add pre-cooked onions and green peppers. When mixture has begun to bubble again, add the slightly beaten eggs, stirring all the while. Remove from the stove immediately and this will result in a smooth, flowing sauce.

Why call it lobster sauce when there is not a lobster in sight? Just because it is the same sauce that lobster is often cooked in. This is especially excellent poured over bowls of hot steamed rice.

OPTIONAL:

2 scallions could be substituted for the bulb onion. If so, add with the cornstarch mixture. A rib of celery, diagonally sliced, can be pre-cooked like the green peppers and added to the sauce. It helps to stretch the portions somewhat. This recipe does not serve too many, probably 2 or 3 persons only. This can be safely doubled, in which case, I use only 3 eggs instead of 4 eggs. Actually, whites only of the eggs are used if one wishes

to be authentic. However, I am quite practical because usually even with the best of intentions I end up wasting the yolks, so I put in whole eggs to begin with.

Lobster (raw) can be used. Chop into bite size chunks leaving the lobster unshelled. Proceed with the lobster the same as the shrimp above. It is quite proper to "slurp" the flavorsome gravy from the red shells of the lobster when eating. Then, remove the shell and enjoy. A combination of crab, shrimp and lobster works nicely, too.

The black bean *dow see* flavor is something that grows on you and the first time you may not quite like it as well as you will eventually. It is a characteristic Chinese flavor and one that is much coveted by the true gourmet. And certainly the flavor cannot be duplicated with any ingredient that is available in the ordinary American supply of flavorings. It is that kind of vibrant and magnificent sauce!

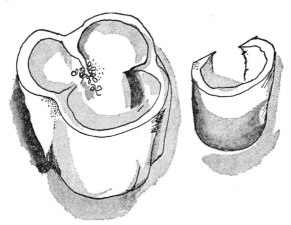

Stuffed Green Peppers With Black Bean Sauce (*Chinese*)

FILLING:

½ lb. shrimp, shelled, deveined and minced	½ tsp. MSG
	1 egg
½ lb. pork (butt, loin, pork chops, etc.), minced	1 green onion, chopped
	¼ tsp. salt
1½ Tbsp. cornstarch	4 or 5 water chestnuts, chopped
1 Tbsp. soy	
1 Tbsp. sherry	

3 medium size good, even-shaped green peppers cut in half crosswise. Remove excess seeds and the stem end. Each half is then cut carefully into sections through the thin membranes inside. You will end up with tiny "pockets" of peppers to be filled. Refer to the sketch for this detail. You will average 6 little peppers from 1 large, well-shaped pepper. If the "pockets" are too large and not uniform, fill them, then slice in half.

Mix filling ingredients together and stuff each piece of green pepper smoothly. Put 1 Tbsp. oil in frying pan, heat to high and put in peppers with filling side down; cover and keep cooking until the pork is done and the pepper is cooked. If necessary, add a little bit of water or stock to help steam-cook the stuffing. Turn the peppers so all sides are nicely browned in the fat, usually this takes about 10 to 15 minutes cooking time. The peppers should be rather on the firm side, preferably not mushy.

BLACK BEAN SAUCE:

1 clove garlic, minced fine	1 tsp. cornstarch
1½ to 2 tsp. fermented salted black beans, washed, drained and mashed	dash of MSG and salt
	1 tsp. sherry
	dash of sugar
1 Tbsp. soy or less	½ cup water

While peppers are cooking, put in a sauce pan about 1 Tbsp. oil, sauté black beans and garlic for ½ minute on high heat. Add the sauce ingredients which have been mixed together and stir until cornstarch is cooked. Pour over peppers and serve. If desired, 1 chili pepper, sliced thin, could be added to the sauce, if this hot spicy taste is to your liking.

VARIATIONS:

This filling is excellent for Japanese dried black mushrooms (*shiitake*) that have been reconstituted in water. Remove the stem and fill the caps. Bitter melon can be sliced in ½-inch slices (boil for 5 minutes to remove some of the bitterness) and the cavity in the center filled with this mixture. Mature cucumbers with seeds removed could be sliced and filled, as could vegetables like zucchini squash, eggplant, or large carrots hollowed out and sliced thick—use your imagination!

You can make regular meat balls with this filling and use only one green pepper, cut in chunks, as a flavoring and accent vegetable while cooking the meat. Pour sauce over all.

Form the miniature pepper "pockets" as above and use your favorite meat loaf mixture for the filling—fine for *hors d'oeuvres.*

Refer to "How to Use Chicken Wings" recipe and use the above recipe to fill one portion of the wing. Call it "Stuffed Wings." Pour bean sauce over all.

BEAN CAKE, RICE, PICKLES

SOY BEAN CURD CAKE

Soy bean cake, soy bean curd cake, *tofu* (Japanese), or *dow fu* (Chinese) are all one and the same product. It is really like a very bland cheese made from soy milk which in turn is a product of soy beans. It takes on whatever flavor it is being cooked with and is called the "boneless meat" of the Orient.

Many of my students have no mental blocks about cooking and eating foods like an Oriental would have, so they come up with more uses for soy bean cake—some of the most unorthodox ways. I cannot vouch for any of them because I have preconceived ideas as to how I like to eat *tofu*. One woman told of bringing bean cake to work along with a can of fruit cocktail. Mix the two together for lunch—something like cottage cheese and fruit! Another mixed the cold *tofu* with her morning cereal, sugar and milk for breakfast. Because of the very high protein content some have been crumbling it up and blending it into stew gravy. This way, even if the children do not like the texture of bean cake (what's that odd looking food?), they benefit from its nutritional value when it's all combined with the flavored gravy. This last suggestion I feel is a good one since it is no different from the way Orientals cook with bean cake and meat and vegetables just like stew.

If you ever have a piece left over and do not know what to do with it, you can mix it up with a meat loaf mixture or add cubes of it into a soup. In fact, in recent years there has been a tremendous increased interest in its high nutritional value.

There is a difference in size between the Japanese type (*tofu*) which is about 3½ inches by 3½ inches by 3½ inches and the Chinese type (*dow fu*) which is firmer and about 1 inch by 3½ inches by 3½ inches.

Any Oriental recipe calling for one Japanese *tofu* is equal to three Chinese *dow fu*. The trouble is one never knows which size is being referred to in the recipe. You will have to use your common sense on this score. In the recipes used in this book I use Japanese size *tofu* since it is more commonly available.

The prices of bean cake keep going up and the sizes seem to be shrinking so what size it will be when you buy it is anyone's guess! I do not recommend expensive canned types or vacuum packed ones from the Orient. The flavor is not very outstanding—in fact, they have an odd flavor. I much prefer the fresh product or omit from the recipe.

One funny incident occurred one day. Someone told me that the uninformed clerk at this supermarket had the idea that the *tofu* might be "alive" since it is always kept in a large can of water, sort of swimming in there like a jelly fish.

Tofu is highly perishable so use it as soon after purchase as you can. Keep it refrigerated in a bowl of fresh water. Change the water often. In a real pinch, in case you cannot use it the day of the purchase or within the next day, put the *tofu* in a saucepan and simmer it with water covered to the top. Cook for about 15 minutes to kill the bacterial action that may be starting. This will preserve the *tofu* for another day or so. It does harden it somewhat, but, usually, you cook it anyway.

To visit a *tofu*-making shop is quite interesting. There are some in the larger cities like San Francisco, San Jose and Los Angeles. The *tofu* is actually the soy milk that is thickened.

Soy milk aside from being a substitute for milk can be used to make your laundry white! The soy bean is a miracle source for industry, agriculture, commerce and nutrition, having hundreds of uses with more being researched all the time.

The versatile soy bean has been cultivated in the Orient for 5,000 years. Only in this century has it become an important crop and appreciated in the United States. Most unique in nutritive value, it contains a much higher proportion of protein and fat than do other legumes, but it also has a lower carbohydrate content.

Green soybeans, if available, can be boiled in salted water.

Clean well to remove any grit that clings to the fuzzy skins. Cover and boil until tender, pods and all. Salt. Serve in pods. Either pull pods between teeth or shell and eat beans only.

A most diversified bean. Lecithin is another important substance derived from soy beans, and it finds a wide application in the candy making industry as an ingredient in chocolate coatings. Lecithin is also the material that is used for aerosol spraying on pans for "no stick" frying without calories.

How to Make Soy Bean Cake (Tofu)

This recipe is not what one would use to make a commercial bean cake but can be used at home for an experiment or if you live so far from a source of fresh bean cake and desire it occasionally. I spent many hours trying to get just the right results. Our family ate an awful lot of odd *tofu* in shape and texture for days.

This home method is quite inexpensive with soy beans being variously fifteen to twenty-five cents per pound; it is much cheaper in large quantities. Making *tofu* at home, however, is time consuming to do, so, plan it for sometime when you have lots of leisure.

The solidifying agent used by the trade is calcium sulfate. My recipe uses lemon juice. Lemon and calcium sulfate affect the coagulation of the plant casein of the soy bean differently. But, for home use and "for the fun of it" experiments—the quite soft, smooth custard texture as found in the commercial quality is not so important—after all, we are not in business. The taste is there, and besides lemon juice is a lot easier to come by than calcium sulfate in our kitchens! It follows, too, with organic foods theories, using no chemicals. I have learned that magnesium chloride and calcium chloride can also be utilized as coagulants, but again, lemon juice is the simplest for us.

This *tofu* can be used in any recipe using bean cake. The dry residue from squeezing out the soy milk can be used in meat loaves or fried and flavored with soy, sugar, vegetables and shrimp. This residue is free for the asking at the *tofu* shops and is called *okara* (Japanese). It is very simple fare but still quite nutritious!

Soy bean cake does not freeze. A change in texture occurs when soy bean cake is frozen. It gets spongy and has its special uses. *Koyadofu* (Japanese) is the name for the frozen, then dehydrated form of bean cake.

Your Very Own Homemade Bean Cake—
Noncommercial Type

1 cup dried soy beans	5 Tbsp. lemon juice (I use the
4 cups water	bottled kind—very handy)

Soak beans in water overnight (10 hours in winter) otherwise 5 hours is sufficient. Drain. Wash beans well. Take about ½ cup soaked beans and 1 cup water. Put in the blender and liquefy for 2 minutes. Place a cheesecloth over a colander to strain the liquid from the liquefied beans. Keep doing this process until all the soaked beans have been put through the blender. Return pulp to blender and add water to cover. Blend for 2 minutes and strain this into original bowl of liquid from beans. This milk-like liquid is soy milk, a very excellent milk, especially recommended for allergy and for special diets.

Boil this milk mixture, stirring carefully since there is a tendency for it to scorch. When it comes to a full boil, add the lemon juice. Stir just enough to blend well with milk. Remove from heat. The liquid will begin to coagulate into a thick, lumpy mixture. As it settles a yellow liquid will rise to the surface. Put this thick mixture into a cloth-lined container with some sort of holes for the liquid to escape. In the trade, a wooden box with perforated walls is used. Keep a slight weight over "cheese" in mold. The idea is to compress it just enough to remove the excess juices but to keep the bean cake in a firm shape, yet not to compress so much that it becomes too dry. Try using a strainer lined with a cheesecloth for a mold or several plastic strawberry baskets nested together for strength and lined with cloth will work. Let the *tofu* set for awhile in the warm water in the mold.

Remove the form carefully and leave the *tofu* still encased in the cloth. Simmer for about 10 to 15 minutes covered with water, it helps to hold the shape. Drain. Keep in refrigerator covered with fresh water. Highly perishable. Change the water often. I advise using it in a few days.

Do not expect a professional bean cake result, but one quite similar and with good flavor. The texture will be a little different.

Bean Cake Delicious (Cold)

Fresh *tofu,* just as purchased and cut into serving portions. Serve on shaved ice bed garnished with soy and flakes of shaved bonito fish (*katsuobushi*), chopped green onions and grated ginger. A dash of MSG does enhance the flavor.

This is especially good cold and refreshing during the hot summer months. *Tofu* offers low calories, and high protein content and excellent health food, but definitely for those with an acquired taste for *tofu* plain. I advise trying bean cake other ways first for the uninitiated.

As a youngster, I remember often eating *tofu.* I made a hole in the center of my *tofu* serving, poured in the soy and made a puncture on the side with a chopstick to watch the soy ooze out. I used to call it a "swimming hole." My folks must have been disgusted with me.

TEA (JAPANESE AND CHINESE)

Tea comes from a plant belonging to the camellia family. The differences of the many types of tea are due to the variations in the locale, in the climate, in the time of harvest and in the general processing of the tea leaves. There are endless varieties resulting in excellent to poor tea qualities.

Actually, green tea (unfermented type) and black tea (such as *oolong* and fermented types), which is sometimes referred to as red tea due to the color, are from the same tea plant.

Genmai Tea (Japanese)

This is a green tea mixed with roasted sweet rice grains (brown in color and some of them are "popped" like white popcorn). The bag of popped rice is usually buried in the bottom so remove it and mix with the green tea leaves before using or you will have green tea leaves almost used up when you come across the rice bag. This tea is rather sweet, nutty and most pleasurable —a very delicate flavor with your meals since it is not overpowering. A good tea!

One condescending student told me that she would pick the "popcorn" out of the tea for me. "No, no," I said, "we want it in there!" That popped rice is what contributes to the delicate flavor of this special home-style tea.

Green Tea (Japanese)

Pure green tea is my all-round favorite for Japanese meals or for serving to company at tea time. There are all kinds of qualities, so buy the best that you can afford. Ask the Orientals what they consider their choice.

Oolong Tea (Chinese)

This is the tea that you most frequently find with Chinese meals when you go to the restaurants and the one that you as a family will enjoy the most with your Chinese foods.

Please do not feel that you must have green tea with Japanese meals alone or vice versa with the *oolong* tea and Chinese meals. You can enjoy either meal with whichever pleases you, or as sometimes is the case, what you have on hand.

I find that the perfumed teas are best left until you become more expert. They have certain fragrances such as jasmine, roses, chrysanthemum and orange blossoms and they often interfere with the taste buds when one does not know about them. You can be shocked at meeting with such flavors and perfumes when you have a certain conception of tea flavor. Perfumed teas are better suited for your snacks, tea time and desserts.

All these teas are served in true Oriental manner without sugar, cream or lemon, but certainly, if you want some additional flavor indulge! The simplest and easiest way to make tea is with tea bags. If using loose tea, about 1 rounded teaspoon equals 1 tea bag. I like to use 1 tea bag in a medium-size tea pot with about 3 to 4 cups of boiling water. Steep for 3 minutes before serving. The 1 tea bag per cup as stated on the tea boxes is just too strong, for me, that is.

Most Orientals enjoy their tea weak rather than strong. But definitely this is optional, and you can have your beverage as you like it—dark and thick or light and thin.

You may like to save tea bags for 1 cup, then another cup and then even another cup. In fact, the later infusions with hot water are considered by some to be the choicest flavor as compared to the original tea from the leaves.

RICE

The easiest way to cook rice to perfection is with an electric automatic rice cooker. Use the measurements given below. Put rice and water in inner pan, then press the button and presto!—all will be ready, never burned and always perfect grains. This cooker eliminates all the guesswork.

As a note: Orientals do not use salt in their rice. If you so desire, you can go ahead and flavor with some salt. The main reason for making it so tasteless (to the uninitiated) is that the gravy and sauces from the various entrees give the rice a taste while you eat it.

Rice (Chinese)

Texas patna long grain rice is the Chinese-type. This is a dry kind and very flaky after cooking if cooked with the correct proportion of water—otherwise, it will be just as gummy and sticky as the Japanese type. Use 2 cups long grain rice to 2½ cups of water. If the rice comes in clear plastic bags or regular boxed packages directly from the distributing source, you rarely have to wash it since it is nice and clean already. However, if it is long grain rice and it appears that the local grocer has made up the packages dividing from a larger sack, then I would suggest that you wash it to remove any dust particles that may be mixed with it. Cook over medium heat without a cover until all the water is absorbed. It will be boiling away. Stir the rice occasionally at this point to distribute the grains. Put a cover on now and turn the heat down to the lowest point. Continue cooking for at least 30 minutes more. Mix carefully before serving. Makes about 4 cups of cooked rice.

This is the best rice for making fried rice. Use the rice cold when preparing, or you will have mushy fried rice.

Rice (Japanese)

Use shorter medium grain "Rose" types, stickier than Chinese-style. This rice must be washed before using since there is a chalky coating of glucose and talc on the surface of the grains. Rub between palms of hands in plenty of water. Wash in cold water and drain until water is clear. Measure 1 cup rice to 1 cup water. This can be allowed to soak 1 hour before cooking, if desired. Cook rice in heavy bottomed pan. Cover. Start with high heat and when water bubbles over, put flame down very low and continue cooking for about 15 to 20 minutes.

Allow to steam. Cool for another 5 to 10 minutes after removing from the stove—leave the cover on. Do not peek! Try to cook small batches of this rice, i.e. 3 cups or so—not 6 cups at a time. Your result will be much more satisfactory. DO NOT stir this rice during the cooking process as you do for the Chinese-style method! Mix carefully before serving to fluff up the kernels loosely. The main thing with this rice is do not *peek* during the cooking process.

Note: With electric stoves, it is wise to use one burner to cook high and then use another burner to cook low so the heat change will be immediate. With gas burners you do not have this heat retention problem.

To resteam rice: Using leftover rice, put a small quantity of water, a few tablespoons, on low heat with a cover until heated through. Or, place the rice cooker pan in your rice cooker and push the button. It will steam nicely with the few spoonfuls of water that you put in the pot.

Japanese Rice Balls

Use unseasoned Japanese-style rice, i.e., no vinegar. Wet hands and salt slightly. Put about ¾ cup *hot* cooked rice on palm of left side. Close it slightly so rice will form a sort of cup. Make a hollow, if you desire, to fill the center. You can use anything for the filling. Pickles, meat or whatever you wish. Now shape the rice into a ball, a triangle or oblong by the way you form your right hand over this mound of rice. Make balls firm so that they will not fall apart. Toasted black sesame seeds sprinkled on the balls give an excellent taste. Toasted flavored *nori* seaweed can be placed on the outer edge of the ball. There is a special kind called *aji-tsuke* (flavored) *nori* that come in little rectangular pieces already toasted.

This *nigiri* (literally translated means fist) is a simple Japanese version of a rice sandwich. This rice ball can be left unfilled and eaten with *teriyaki* meats and such at picnics, hot or cold.

Okai (Japanese)

This is sort of a Japanese rice gruel and wonderful especially when one is not feeling up to eating much; i.e. illness, upset stomach, too much holiday heavy foods, or really any time. You *certainly* do not have to get sick to eat it!

Boil a quart of water, salt slightly and add a cup of cooked Japanese rice or use ½ cup of uncooked, washed rice. Simmer until it gets very soft, soupy and creamy. Very similar to Chinese *jook* or *congee*. A bowl of this *okai* and weak green tea plus a few pieces of salted vegetables or *umeboshi* (salted red preserved plums) have a sort of curing effect and, here again, there is without a doubt nothing like it in American foods with any similarity. This appeals to the palate when you feel like eating nothing else. You get nourishment and the *okai* is easy to digest; and no work to chew except for the red salted Japanese plums that you may find far too salty and impossible!

I have known people to go visit their sick ones in hospitals and sneak in this combination, knowing that the patient hasn't been eating but would "down" this favorite of his.

There is a specially cured Chinese salted dried plum with sugar and licorice added that is considered to be a "cold" and "sore throat" cure. Eat one and your sickness disappears. I've heard it works! You can take it from there.

Rice O-Chazuke (Japanese)

O-chazuke is rice with tea (Japanese) poured over it. This rice and tea with broiled salted salmon (*shake*—Japanese) soaked in *sake* lees and some pickles is delicious! There is no comparison to any food combination in America. The imported, salted salmon is sold commercially in small packets in many of the Oriental food stores and is very expensive. You may wish to try making your own. Very easy . . . if you have the fresh salmon and can secure the *sake* lees.

Salmon Soaked in Sake Lees

This is delectable and exhilarating. Make a mixture of 2 cups *sake* lees (*kasu*) and 1 cup sugar. *Kasu* is the residue remaining in the production of rice wine, so don't overdo it, too much can get one a bit "woozy."

Cut 1½ to 2 lbs. fresh salmon into serving pieces. Salt well on both sides with sack type pickling salt. Set aside in bowl for 4 or 5 days in refrigerator. Drain well. Do not wash the fish. The pieces will be rather firm and hard since much of the liquid has been removed. Dry with paper towels. Cover salmon slices with the above *sake* lees mixture. Put in a container. The seasoned fish will be ready-to-eat in about 10 days after proper preparation. Keep covered in the refrigerator. It will keep for months. Wipe off most of the coating of lees and broil until the fish flakes (about 10 to 15 minutes). Remember, it is quite salty. One can partake of only so much! The *sake* gives the salmon that marvelous flavor that is truly delicious.

Oriental Pickles

It is believed that the typical pickles that we see in Japanese cuisine really originated in China. They have similar salted, sweet and sour greens, turnips and so on. The Chinese, however, use their pickles basically in cooked dishes—salting to pickle vegetables is a way of preserving food for winter use. The Japanese use theirs primarily as an appetizer-type vegetable pickle at the table to go with rice. They follow the seasons and pickle what is available at that particular time.

The art of pickling Japanese-style is slowly disappearing in America so in this section you will find a few of my most treasured recipes. These can be prepared with ease in the American home.

There are so many kinds of pickles. Some are preserved in *sake* lees (this is the residue remaining from the preparation of rice wine), salt, bran, mustard and so on. Every family has its favorite flavorings and secrets. Commercially, many kinds are sold in jars, cans, vacuum sealed plastic containers and some loose in large tubs. These days the "big tub" style is too odoriferous for a modern spic and span supermarket to handle in the States. They are generally a bit saltier and sometimes sweeter, to suit every consumer.

I have discovered the following to be most appealing to the uninitiated. *Tokyozuke* or *fukujinzuke* (Japanese) is very popular since it is rather a sweet taste blended with soy and has a very crunchy texture. The unfamiliar vegetables are of very peculiar shapes so everyone finds it all the more intriguing.

Rakkyo (Japanese) is a pickled scallion and very much like our sweet pickles. This onion does not leave any sort of onion taste and if given a chance, many a person could easily go through a jar in quick order. Makes excellent appetizers, entirely different from the little white onions we see on the gourmet shelf at the market. These are very light beige in color and shaped like the bottom end of a green onion but larger in size. Wrap a slice of canned abalone and keep together, the pickled scallion and the abalone, with toothpicks. What luscious eating!

Every pickle maker has his own recipe so discover certain brands and stick with them. One of the most used vegetables in Japanese pickles as well as in much of the Japanese cuisine and in limited amount by the Chinese is the *daikon* (radish). Both roots and tops are utilized. *Daikon* is rich in diastase which is an enzyme that changes starches into maltose and later into dextrose. Diastase is therefore a good digestive aid and relieves a person who may have had just too much rice or other starchy foods. The one objection you may find in using fresh *daikon* is the smell. It is rather strong but if you know what it is, you will not find it is objectionable. This is true with many of the radish family as you probably know.

The Chinese have a sweet white cucumber sold in cans. It is often used to garnish sweet and sour sauce dishes as well as being just nibbled on with rice. There is another mixture called sweet mixed ginger that comes in cans. This is Chinese and does not include just ginger but vegetables too. This is a mixture that is often used in the sauce of *sub gum* entrees. This is by no means a complete summary of all the kinds of pickles there are in Oriental cuisine. I only have mentioned the more common types.

Takuwan—Yellow Radish Pickles (Japanese)

3 cups water	2 cups sugar
1 cup vinegar (regular apple or pineapple cider vinegar)	¾ cup salt (pickling type in sacks, not ice cream salt)

Boil water. Add vinegar and boil for a few minutes. Add sugar and simmer for 15 minutes. *Slowly* add the salt before turning off heat. Stir to dissolve. Cool off about 1 minute and place this solution into mason jars that have been sterilized and already filled with dried *daikon*.

The above syrup is enough for about 2 or 3 quarts filled with dried *daikon*. Do not pack too tightly. Remember the *daikon* will swell up after standing.

How to Dry Daikon (Japanese Radish)

Wash *daikon*. Scrub with brush if a lot of dirt is imbedded in skin. Do not peel. Leave tops on for easy drying and remove just before use. Dry outside in sunshine. A clothesline is ideal. Drape *daikon* over line and leave in hot sun 3 or 4 days. Forget what your neighbors think, remember how delicious it will taste! Rinse off lightly with water to clean off dust particles. Do not soak in water. Discard tops. The *daikon* should be limp but not completely dehydrated, just as if you had left a carrot out of the refrigerator on the drain board for a few days—rather a limp, pliable root.

Pack either in chunks or slices into sterilized jars. Pour hot syrup and tighten mason lids. This is considered sealed enough. It's a good idea to do this job outside on the barbecue table so that the smells can drift into the atmosphere! Allow to stand in a cool, dark place about 1 month. The color will change to a deep yellow naturally—ready to devour to your heart's delight. If desired, you could add a chili pepper in each jar before putting in syrup. This pickle has a very pungent odor when ready to serve so be prepared. Do not let the smell stop you from tasting it, you will become an addict like the rest of us.

Salted Pickles With Nappa (Japanese)

Cut a head of Chinese *nappa* cabbage into quarters (into eighths, if large). Salt lightly with 2 Tbsp. pickling salt—not the shaker salt that we use for our daily table use, but the type in small paper sacks. Put in a large, deep bowl or crock. Put 4 or 5 dried prunes or ¼ cup raisins and 1 cup water on cabbage. Mix well so that the salt will be dissolved. The prunes and raisins help to cut the very sharp, salty taste that is often common in pickles, and give a slight, sweet desirable flavor, too.

Put a weight on *nappa*. A large pot full of water on a plate serves as a good weight. In some families they have a huge "pickle rock" used just for this purpose. The rock is placed on top of a wooden plate so the pressure will be equalized. You could do that. Be sure to scrub your heavy rock very well before using.

Leave weight until water rises. Usually, it will be ready-to-eat after 12 to 15 hours of soaking. Wash off *nappa* a little bit. Discard the raisins. Slice or chop *nappa* into bite sizes. Squeeze out any additional water. Flavor with MSG and soy. A little lemon juice and grated fresh ginger mixed with a bit of sugar gives a good optional flavor. You can keep this pickle a few days and, if you wish to preserve it longer without getting sour, place it in a jar with a cover. Leave in the refrigerator.

If, by chance, it does get too sour for your taste, it can be "laundered" or washed out in a bowl of water. Then squeezed dry and cut into tiny pieces for serving with soy and MSG.

This pickle clears the mouth of any after tastes from a meal and is quite refreshing.

Pickle Mash (Japanese)

This is a pickle base for soaking vegetables for a very special, simple but satisfying, and most refreshing pickle. *Dobu zuke* (Japanese) would be the plain peasant-type word for this type of pickle, but leave it not just to the rural folks, city people love it as much.

Mix 3 cups leftover rice (especially suited to Japanese shorter-grain rice) with one bottle of beer. Allow this to stand in refrigerator for 3 or 4 days. Add a little more leftover rice daily, mixing well to permit aeration. I like to add a small handful of salt and half of a handful of sugar to the mixture. A few pieces of fresh ginger gives a tangy flavor.

Add freshly washed vegetables which have had salt sprinkled on them. Cucumbers, regular cabbage (our cannon ball type), *nappa* cabbage, *daikon* (radish), turnips, celery, cauliflower, broccoli and eggplant work very well in this mash. Keep this mash well mixed daily.

Leave the vegetables in the mixture for at least 2 days, or until wilted, and wash a piece to sample. If salted enough to suit your taste, remove what you desire for the one meal. Wash rice off. Cut into pleasant, bite-size morsels. Serve with Japanese meals with soy.

Use repeatedly. But be sure to give the mash a stir with the hands daily. This keeps up the fermented condition of the rice. Add more leftover rice as you have some to add. (The principle is like your "starter" for yeast breads. Once the molds have begun, you can keep going for quite awhile before starting fresh again.)

Salted Greens—Kim Chee (Korean)

Many Oriental meals include this *Kim Chee* as a sort of appetizer and, once the taste craze is acquired, despite the redolent odor and its permeating quality, there is no stopping. The first taste or two may not even turn you on. It took me a number of years before I actually began to adore the pickle.

1 medium head of Chinese *nappa* cabbage	½ tsp. grated ginger root
½ cup pickling salt	2 stalks of green onions, either chopped or left in 1½-inch lengths
4 cups water	
1 tsp. crushed dry red pepper	½ tsp. salt
1 or 2 cloves garlic, finely minced	1½ tsp. sugar
	dash of MSG

Wash the cabbage and cut into ¾-inch lengths. Add salt and water. Soak for about 1 hour. Drain and rinse the cabbage well. Add red pepper, garlic, ginger, green onions, and the remaining ingredients. Press down into a mason jar, cover and refrigerate for at least 2 or 3 days to "ripen" and become slightly sour.

You could leave it out at room temperature for 2 days and the process will be hastened a bit. All in all, it is a rather smelly business, this fermentation, but terribly rewarding once the inclination to eat it becomes yours. Don't be dismayed when I tell you that there are people who make this by the gallons at one time. You may wish to dip the pickle into soy as you eat. If you are hesitant about so much pepper, garlic, and so on, try this variation. Put the garlic clove on a toothpick. Leave the green onions in long lengths and knot it into a big wad. These two procedures will help you remove them from the jar after a few days. Use a smaller amount of chili or leave it out. Leaving out these flavors altogether from the recipe would not result in a true *kim chee* taste. Koreans even add shrimp and other seafoods for variety. I'll take mine as in the recipe without these embellishments!

Easy Turnips (Japanese)

Slice very sheer, unpeeled turnips. Salt slightly and toss in bowl to coat salt evenly. After about 10 to 15 minutes, with your hands stir and press down on turnips. Compress to remove excess water. Drain. Serve loosened up a bit. A very quick way to have *tsukemono* (Japanese) or "soaked things" with your meal. Serve with soy and a dash of MSG.

Crunchy Land and Sea Pickles (Japanese)

2 chili peppers
1 cup soy
1 (4 oz.) pkg. *kiri konbu* (dried kelp or seaweed)
1 (3 oz.) pkg. *hanagiri daikon* (dried white radish which looks rather beige color in the package)
⅓ cup Japanese rice wine vinegar (increase, if you desire more acid taste)
2 tsp. MSG
1¼ cup sugar

Boil together the chili peppers, soy, vinegar, MSG and sugar. Wash the *konbu* and the *daikon* well and squeeze dry. Place in syrup mixture and boil for 5 minutes.

Remove the *daikon* and the *konbu* to cool onto a plate. Heat syrup to boiling without the vegetables. Allow the mixture to cool. Then, combine with the *konbu* and the *daikon* before putting in a jar. Cover and keep refrigerated. Toasted sesame seeds could be added just before serving as an accompaniment to rice. This keeps quite a long time in the refrigerator and is handy when you want a little something with rice and tea.

Is There Something to the Wisdom of the Ancestors?

By the use of rusty, old iron nails in salting vegetables, such as deep purple colored egg plants, the Japanese thought is that they will help to retain the natural colorings instead of bleaching them out. I cannot get myself to use old nails, but I understand this works—the chemical reaction of the iron, I imagine. I've also heard this mentioned about cooking Japanese style sweet black dried beans. Put in a few nails and the black color will remain intact.

DESSERTS

ABOUT SWEET DESSERTS IN THE SHOPS

In most of the larger cities there are certain areas that are considered Japanese town or Chinatown. These towns identify city locations and do not necessarily mean where all the Orientals reside. Most of them are well integrated now and many live in the suburbs, except in San Francisco where there is still a dense Chinese population in the Grant Avenue area.

There are all kinds of different shops, very foreign to our probing eyes. One of them is the Oriental confectioner. In the Chinese shops you will see moon cakes, pretzels, fried rice cakes, almond cookies, donuts, date treats, licorice-ginger strips for nibbling, salted plums, watermelon seeds, lichee nuts, sesame and peanut candies, and on and on.

In the Japanese stores there are rice crackers and cookies, bean jelly, *manju,* tea cakes with glutinous rice coverings, some with beautiful, pale-colored artistic designs and assorted fillings. Some shops are outstanding for their aesthetically designed pastries. I know persons from New York who stop while on the West Coast to purchase specialties made at a particular Japanese confectioner because their products excel.

Do not let the visual beauty of Oriental goodies betray you. Many do not appeal to Americans at first, or never will. Some may take years to grow on you and yet you may like some immediately. Some look like chocolate filling and you can imagine what a terrific let-down, to discover sweetened red beans. Usually, tea is served with these assorted specialties. Some are available only at certain festival times.

The Orientals were original in their use of sweetened beans

in making this type of dessert. You do not find this in your European foods, probably because in the Orient there was little use of dairy products, that is, cream and butter. But now there is a change taking place and in Japan, especially, heavy, rich French pastries are at their finest. Gradually, high cholesterol is invading the Far East as it has here in America.

DESSERTS FOR ORIENTAL MEALS AND AS SNACKS

We Americans have a tendency toward desserts—the Orientals, especially the Chinese, do not go for too many sweets. The Japanese seem to prefer them. With their usual dinners, however, the Japanese and the Chinese often serve fruits or no dessert at all. We find this true in the United States now that so much emphasis is being placed on weight loss control, low calories, polyunsaturated fats, organic fruits and vegetables. This is good.

The Japanese and Chinese have some similar desserts. They both use glutinous rice flour, sometimes called sweet rice flour (*nor mai fun* in Chinese and *mochiko* in Japanese) for making desserts. They have a very similar dish made with fruits and rice flour dumplings. This has some resemblance to large size tapioca "blobs."

Fruit Shiratama (Japanese)

2 cups glutinous sweet rice   1 cup water
    flour (*mochiko*)

Pour water on flour and mix to make a soft dough. Shape into ½-inch balls and then flatten hollow in center. Put into boiling water. When they float up to the surface remove and place in cold water to cool.

Take the juice from canned mandarin oranges and pineapple and add about 1 cup water (depends upon amount of juices available). Add ¾ cup of sugar and dissolve in liquid while you bring it to boil. When cool, add ½ tsp. rum or whatever flavoring you wish. Put the drained, cooled balls in a large glass bowl. Pour the cooled fruit juices and the fruits in. A few ice cubes could be added at this point.

Sweet Orange Tea (Chinese)

4 to 5 Tbsp. glutinous sweet rice
   flour

Add water 1 tsp. at a time to make stiff paste. Form small
⅜-inch balls. Bring about 2½ cups of water to a boil. Stir in ¾
cup sugar to dissolve. Drop rice balls in sugared water and continue to boil until they float and are soft. Stir in 3 oranges which
have been seeded and segmented with the membranes removed.
Also, add any juice that might have spilled while you were getting the pulp ready. The segments should be broken into small
pieces. Cook mixture now only to heat through. Serve hot in small
bowls. One could substitute 4 or 5 tangerines or tangelos for the
oranges.

Sweet Bean Dessert

Both the Japanese and the Chinese use cooked red beans,
sweetened and wrapped in dough then steamed or baked for a
pastry sweet. This is not generally served at the end of the meal
but as an in-between-meal snack with tea.

Chinese Steamed Rice Dessert

3 Tbsp. solid vegetable shortening, melted, for filling
1 cup canned prepared sweetened bean paste (or make
   your own bean paste
   from red *azuki* beans and
   sugar)

1 cup chopped dates
2 or 3 Tbsp. sesame seeds or
   chopped walnut meats
   (optional)

Melt shortening, add bean paste, dates and mix. Cook over
low heat stirring constantly for 5 to 8 minutes. Cool. When cold
make 30 ¾-inch size balls of this bean mixture. Set aside.

3 cups glutinous sweet rice
   flour
1½ cups water (approximately)
3 Tbsp. white corn syrup
3 Tbsp. sugar

3 Tbsp. solid vegetable shortening (optional, although
   this does help to keep
   the dough soft after
   steaming)

Mix together flour and water in bowl with all other ingredients (syrup, sugar and shortening). Texture will be like pastry or biscuit dough consistency. Form a big ball—from this pinch off and shape 30 walnut-size balls. Flatten out the balls, keeping the center thicker than the edges, about 1½ inches in diameter. Put the bean and date ball in the center of the patty. Carefully bring the edges up and pinch together to form a sort of pouch. Roll between the palms of the hands carefully to form a smooth ball surface.

Place on foil squares. Do not put too close together since they do swell somewhat. Steam in vigorous steam until translucent in appearance, about 12 to 15 minutes. Sprinkle angel flake coconut shreds over buns while hot or you can dip the buns into the coconut. Can be served hot or cold, but better served hot since the outer rice skin remains more tender. If desired, one can make ahead and steam again just before serving.

Steamed Cake (Chinese)

The Japanese and the Chinese both have steamed cakes, since ovens are lacking in many homes the steaming method became the way to bake their cake. The Japanese version is called *kasutera*. Here is a recipe called Sponge Cake but it is not quite like the true American style baked sponge cake. It is moister and a common cake in China.

4 eggs, separated	½ tsp. baking powder
⅞ cup powdered sugar	½ tsp. vanilla
1 cup sifted cake or regular flour	½ tsp. almond extract

Beat egg whites stiff. Add sugar gradually. Continue beating until stiff peaks form. Add beaten yolks and blend. Fold in flour and baking powder which have been sifted together. Add the extracts. Place batter in a 9-inch paper-lined cake pan. (Cut out a piece of wax paper to fit the bottom only.) Steam for 15 minutes or more until done. Press surface and when it springs back it should be removed from steamer. The surface will be wet-looking and colorless as far as browning goes. For a make-shift steamer use an electric skillet. Put water in pan almost to top edge. Elevate the cake pan with empty tuna fish cans or something so that it will be above the water level. Cover tightly. Be sure water is boiling before putting cake in steamer. If using a regular steamer and there is room, use a clean dish towel just under the cover to prevent droplets of water from falling on the cake surface.

Good served warm.

This is a very plain cake and can be glamorized by adding whipped cream. Also good for a strawberry shortcake base. Crystallized ginger, cut up fine, and folded into whipped cream makes Oriental cake. This is an easy way to prepare cake and on a hot day it is a life saver; do it out on the patio using an electric skillet.

AMERICANIZED ORIENTAL DESSERTS

The fortune cookie is an Oriental-American confectioner's dream, especially, with all of those "lucky-good-prosperous-happy" fortunes! I had some recently that had philosophical Chinese sayings, quite sophisticated and most unusual. Here is a sample: "Of a truth, men are mystically united: a mystic bond of brotherhood makes all men one."

In large cities like San Francisco and Los Angeles, you can actually order fortune cookies with your own clever sayings enclosed. There are specialty shops in these Chinatowns. Some of them even offer guided tours of their factories.

At one recent wedding I attended, *haiku* poems were written by a relative and dedicated to the bride and groom in each dessert fortune cookie at the nuptial party. Another fantastic idea that I heard publicized: at a grand opening of a hotel in Chinatown— a giant fortune cookie was broken and out stepped two lovely Oriental girls. Take it from here, dear reader, and think of your own idea!

Icy Citrus Ginger

Surround a scoop of lemon or lime sherbet with a few canned mandarin orange sections on a sparkling crystal dessert dish.

Sprinkle with tiny bits of crystallized ginger and a pinch of grated orange peel. Pour fresh orange juice over the sherbet and garnish with chopped nuts.

Fruits Combined With Ginger

Mandarin oranges combined with bits of crystallized ginger and lichee nuts.

Pineapple chunks and mandarin oranges marinated in ginger-ale. Served icy-cold.

Cut bananas in half. Cover with chopped, preserved ginger and sprinkle with 1 Tbsp. ginger syrup. Serve with whipped cream or vanilla ice cream.

Ginger Ice Cream

Some ice cream makers now have available on the market exotic fruit flavored ice creams. Of them all, ginger is the all-time favorite. It is becoming more and more available in larger cities. Among some of the other fancies are mango, guava, and green tea flavors.

You can achieve a sort of ginger ice cream by softening vanilla ice cream and adding a bit of crystallized ginger, chopped very fine. Refreeze. Make it with just a touch of the exotic flavor. Give it your own personalized exotic name.

Ginger Candy

Cut thin slivers of preserved-type ginger or crystallized ginger and dip in melted milk chocolate. Allow to harden on wax paper.

Sweet Ginger Relish

A preserved ginger that is packed in jars with sugar and honey. It is most delicate and fairly mild as an appetizer, dessert, meat and fowl complement, cake and ice cream topping.

Agar-Agar—Kanten—Dessert (Japanese)

Agar-agar or *kanten* is used in many foods that we might not even be aware of, and increasingly in America we are just discovering what the Orientals have known for a long time.

The one advantage of agar-agar over regular unflavored gelatin as we know it, is that it sets at room temperature and does not need refrigeration. By making your regular gelatin salad and adding a quantity of dissolved agar-agar it will hold up at any buffet table without collapsing.

Agar-agar is firm and more rubbery to the bite. It does not have that familiar Jello-quiver. It can also be cut into exact, sharp corners without fear. One of the most interesting uses for agar-agar in the baking industry is that it is now being added to frostings on cakes to prevent the plastic covers from sticking, as for example, a package of cup cakes.

1 stick red *kanten* (Japanese agar-agar)	pinch salt
1 stick white *kanten*	½ cup Hawaiian Punch concentrated base in bottle
4 cups water	1 small can pineapple, crushed
1 cup sugar	juice of 1 lemon

Wash *kanten*. Rinse in cold water. Soak *kanten* in 4 cups of cold water for 30 minutes. Boil until *kanten* melts. Do not cover. Add sugar and salt. Cook 10 to 15 minutes. Add punch base, crushed pineapple and strained lemon juice. Pour *kanten* into a pan which has been rinsed with cold water. Chill. Fills an 8-inch by 12-inch by 2½-inch pan. Serve in slices.

Chinese Almond Cookies

Lard is used in true Chinese cookie baking but I find the substitution of hard vegetable shortenings to be most satisfactory. Do not use an electric beater to mix this cookie batter. The over-creaming results in the cookies flattening out instead of remaining in a nice mound. This is similar to the crackly "Snickerdoodle" cookies and gets puffy in baking.

1 cup solid vegetable shortening or lard
1 cup sugar
1 egg
1 tsp. almond extract
2 cups flour
pinch of salt

¼ tsp. cream of tartar
1 tsp. baking soda
sliced almonds or white sesame seeds
beaten egg for brushing tops of cookies

Cream shortening and sugar until light and fluffy. Mix by hand. Add egg and almond extract and beat well. Sift dry ingredients and add to the creamed mixture. Shape into small balls and place on ungreased cookie sheet. Press top of cookie slightly and brush top with beaten egg. Press sliced almond on center or sprinkle with sesame seeds. Bake in 350° to 375°F. oven for 12 to 15 minutes or until light brown, depending on temperature variance. Medium color is what you want. Do not get too brown. These are very short cookies.

Almond Dowfu Dessert (Chinese)

1 pkg. unflavored gelatin
2 Tbsp. cold water
¾ cup boiling water
4 Tbsp. sugar

1 cup canned evaporated milk or half and half
1½ tsp. almond extract

Dissolve gelatin in cold water. Add boiling water, sugar, milk and extract. Stir and dissolve well. Pour into 9 inch square pan. Refrigerate. When set, dice into ¾-inch cubes. Garnish with maraschino cherries, using the syrup flavored with a few drops of almond extract. (Easy way—put drops into jar and shake around.) Pour over cubes in sauce dishes. A bit of food color can be added if you do not wish white for the gelatin cubes. Do this during the first step before refrigerating. Mandarin orange segments or lichee (canned) or a mixture of cherries and oranges make a nice combination to pour over the cubes. Or, be Americanized and use our ever faithful standby—fruit cocktail for an easy dessert, quite refreshing and not too sweet. *Dowfu* refers to the similarity the gelatin cubes have to bean curd cakes.

Celestial Berries

Use large, bright red well-shaped strawberries uniform in shape. Wash. Leave hulls and stems on. Arrange 6 or 7 berries on each glass plate. Place a mound of powdered (sifted) sugar in the center. To eat, hold the stems and dip in the sugar—a most delectable and picturesque ending to any Oriental meal!

BEAUTIFUL PERSIMMONS—KAKI (JAPANESE)

Here on the West Coast as in the Orient, we have the exotic, bright, deep orange persimmons hanging in abundance like ornaments from barren branches in the fall and winter months. Persimmons are a beautiful sight and certainly an addition to our landscape. However, there are those who know not how to utilize this "gold" in their yards or those displayed in the markets—a most misunderstood and underrated fruit! It is a temptation to eat for the color is so scrumptious, but if you have ever experienced the sharp, puckery aftereffect of an innocent, luscious-looking underripe persimmon, one can understand the hesitancy to use more persimmons.

As an interesting note, it is believed that eating persimmons 30 minutes before imbibing effectively prevents a hangover by reducing the acetaldehyde in the blood (this is the principal cause of a hangover although I'm inclined to think that it is just plain overindulgence).

Persimmons are rich in vitamin C and recognized for their beneficial medicinal properties. The leaves are often made into a tea in the Orient and used for coughs, for reducing blood pressure, and for stomach upsets.

Hachiya Persimmon

There are basically two types of persimmon in the United States. One is the more widely-known and slightly astringent oblong fruit with pointed tip—the *Hachiya* variety. These can be picked while very firm, but already colored, and kept at room temperature until they ripen. Or make a beautiful ornamental table decoration combined with autumn-colored leaves. When fully ripe, the fruit is soft to the touch and it develops a rather translucent look. Enjoy it out of hand or chill, or freeze it partially, and slice (or leave whole) for fruit salad or dessert. Add a little citrus juice to help point up the flavor.

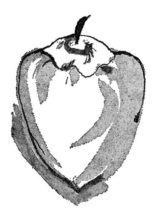

After saying you cannot eat this puckery, astringent fruit except as a soft, ripe fruit—here is a way to consume it firm. You will be pleasantly surprised. Put 5 or 6 hard, orange colored *Hachiya* persimmons in a plastic bag with a ripe apple. Close the bag tight and put it in a dark place like a cupboard. After 5 days the fruit will be edible without puckeriness even though the flesh is fairly firm and the color is still slightly chalky and not quite translucent in appearance. The ethylene gas given off by the ripe apple does the trick. This is a quick way to ripen green bananas, too.

There is still another method of preparing hard *Hachiya* persimmons. Put a few drops of brandy or whiskey into a pin hole made near the calyx. Leave in a dark place wrapped in newspapers or store in a rice bin with uncooked rice grains. Occasionally, the fruit spoils so check often. And it doesn't always work. I personally like the apple method. It is simpler and *always* effective and most reliable!

And, while still on the subject of the magic of apples—you may have grown a pineapple plant from the cut-off top of a pineapple but it has never bloomed. Take your potted plant and place it and a ripe apple in a closed plastic bag. After 4 or 5 days remove the apple and the bag. Continue to take care of the plant in the usual way. Remember that it is a tropical plant and must not be exposed to cold or freezing temperatures. Experts in the know say this method will produce a pineapple bloom within a 6 months' period. As an additional note, it is generally thought that picking persimmons after a touch of frost results in better flavor and both blanching and boiling of persimmons eliminate the possibility of pucker.

Whenever applesauce is used in a recipe, you can generally substitute ripe persimmon pulp with good results.

Fuyu Persimmon

There is another more uncommon variety called *Fuyu*. The fruit is squattier and more like a flat apple. It does not have the pointed tip but is more rounded and flat at the bottom. It can be eaten firm and hard and does not have the puckery astringent effect of the unripe *Hachiya* type. Instead, surprisingly, there is a crunchiness and a special sweetness that makes it truly a different fruit very similar to the mouth-watering flavor of a good Delicious variety apple.

This type of persimmon is not readily available in all markets, but in time, I believe it will become more popular. Once there was a time when no one knew about broccoli, bean sprouts, artichokes, pineapples, mangoes and so on. The ingenious Japanese even use the firm *Fuyu* variety grated (⅔ cup) in a bowl mixed with about 3 Tbsp. rice wine vinegar, 1 tsp. salt (or less), 1 Tbsp. sugar and a dash of MSG mixed together and served as a dressing for a vegetable or fruit salad.

Dried Persimmons

In Japan the versatile golden persimmon fruit is dried, sliced and eaten as a good-tasting confection, much as we munch on raisins. By dehydrating part of the fruit you have effectively preserved some of your crop which in some bumper years produces tremendous yields! The light, barren branches literally droop from the tremendous weight of the persimmons.

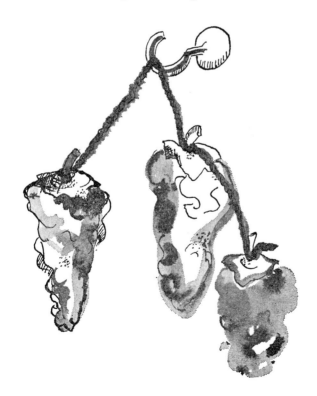

The dried persimmons can be cut up as fruit in place of dates or raisins in baking. The resultant fruit is brownish in color and firmer than dates in texture, rather chewy. This is entirely different from the fresh fruit.

Sun-drying is practical if you have a stretch of hot sunny days. Peel the skin of unbruised, fully colored firm *Hachiya* persimmons. Leave the calyx as a holder. Tie a string firmly to the fruit under the calyx. Tie one fruit, then another, in succession, leaving space so they do not touch. Hang out on a back porch if you are lucky enough to have one these days! Or hang on a clothes line to sun-dry. One could drape a cheesecloth or nylon netting over all so that the insects would not be able to approach the fruits while they are drying. The fruits will very soon begin to shrivel and lose their moist look. Test one by cutting to see if the dehydration is complete; they should be an even reddish-golden brown color throughout the dried fruit and still leathery, not hard and brittle.

Store in an airtight container in the refrigerator or in the freezer. As it ages in the icebox, the dried fruit surface will whiten, just like a dusting of powder. This is an accumulation of its natural sugars.

Freezing Ripe Persimmons

Place fully ripe fruit in plastic container and freeze. Easy to do. Serve partially thawed and sliced as a fruit salad, as a dessert or for baking. The fruit darkens at room temperature so a bit of citrus juices poured over it will help maintain its color.

Anyone familiar with Japan would be most delighted with persimmons as a dessert for an Oriental-type meal.

HELPFUL HINTS

This potpourri section offers a treasury of cultural exchanges, a multitude of odds and ends, and many gold nugget ideas that I want to share with you. Some are humorous, some are old superstitions, some are plain obvious facts while others are at best, just whimsical thoughts. Read as you like—I had great fun putting them together. Many of these came to light over the years, some from experience, some from friends, and some from my students. Some I just plain thought up!

Notes About Storing Foreign Ingredients:

Most things keep best in the refrigerator. Store in tightly covered jars or containers to retain flavors, prevent odors from escaping.

Seaweed, sesame seeds and dried ingredients can best be stored in their containers on your pantry shelf.

Dried mushrooms can be refrigerated in plastic bags for long keeping.

Some items have very strong odors, such as preserved turnip and salted fermented black beans, and should be wrapped in several heavy plastic bags before storing in the refrigerator.

Care should be taken in substituting in Oriental recipes; our regular cabbage is much too strongly flavored to substitute for Chinese cabbage. However, frozen sweet peas may safely substitute for snow peas, edible-pod peas, etc.

Good Ideas While Cooking:

Soak your *teriyaki* wooden skewers in water for 15 minutes before use so they will become water logged and less apt to burn when you broil your *teriyaki*. Saves many a charred skewer as well as leaving a handle for you to hold while you gorge the delectably flavored meat morsels!

Put a bunch of long wooden skewers in a tall container by your fondue pot and they will be handy to spear whatever you have in your pot, especially if it is a buffet-type fondue party.

Use long wooden *teriyaki* skewers to close up the turkey when you stuff the cavity. Weave it back and forth in the skin. Saves threading a big-eyed needle and sewing up the turkey or other fowl when your hands are all slippery from working with turkey.

To open the clear plastic bag of soy bean paste (*miso*) which is enclosed in a cottage cheese type container, cut a small slash at the corner of the plastic bag. To measure: squeeze out right into your measuring spoon or cup what you need just like decorating a cake with a pastry bag.

Cornstarch makes a clear Oriental gravy—not cloudy as in using flour in your sauces. Be sure it is cooked until translucent or it will have a chalky taste.

Use egg roll skins for Italian *cannelloni* and *manicotti* and *won ton* skins for *raviolis*.

Salt is not used in cooking Oriental-style rice. Use it, though, if you like it better that way. After all, you are the one consuming it!

Water measurement for cooking rice is judged by the Orientals by the water level of the rice pot up to the first joint of the middle finger when placed on top of the rice grains. I rarely measure the water by cups when I am home. I use this finger measurement. But sometimes I find I am off and the rice is hard or too soft. Measuring accurately is the safest way but then when you are in a hurry you might like this casual method.

If you wish the rice to cook extra fast, start with boiling water instead of cold water. It will cook faster.

True Chinese cooking uses far more oil than I advise you in this book. I am cooking from a health standpoint and I find I can still maintain good flavors.

Use a rubber spatula with a wooden handle when you cook

the heavy sauces, such as sweet and sour, puddings, etc. You will discover that there is no sticking or scorching if you keep stirring. Scrapes every bit of the goodness from the pan, too— no waste.

Contents of *egg foo young* can vary (as your stew pot does) from time to time. Leftover meat and vegetables could be added very nicely. A lady friend told me that all she had was some left-over corned beef in the refrigerator, so she made "corned beef egg foo young," a la American-Irish-Oriental!

Chicken skin can be removed in any of your Oriental poultry recipes if you desire less fat. The yellow fat is concentrated, especially these days by the rapid feed processes, in the skin. The chickens are getting fat like humans with enriched foods.

In place of mincing pork each time you need it, get a big pork roast. Cut it into small chunks removing excess fat and put through the meat grinder. Grind and grind. Measure into 1 cup portions. Wrap in plastic. Store in a large plastic bag in the freezer. Label. This is not the ideal or the best way since the meat gets mashed and some juices may be lost, but it is far easier than "chop-chop" for me. It is convenient and saves a lot of time thawing out frozen meat and getting ready when time is tight. In fact, you could even slice your meats and label slices and freeze.

No butter or dairy products are used in Oriental cooking except in rare cases. The Chinese use lard; however, I substitute vegetable oils with more successful and healthy results. No olive oil, please.

Use sesame oil only for giving fragrance to dishes instead of frying with it. Measure by drops, not by cups.

The Chinese like the fattier pieces of pork in *char siu* and meat *bows*.

Heat your pan well before adding the oil for Chinese cooking. Slosh it all over the surface. It is this intense heat and oil that seals the juices and cooks the ingredients rapidly without flavor loss. Each minute portion retains its flavor identity.

The faster and harder you scrape on the fine Japanese grater with a Japanese *daikon* radish the hotter and spicier your result- ing juicy gratings (*oroshi*), which is almost like a puree, will be. Try taking the same *daikon* and grating it on a large grater American style. It will be less potent. If these large gratings are too hot for your taste, you can rinse in cold water and drain.

A Chinese meal typically has many "entrees" and everything is shared by the diners serving more people, more dishes and more variety.

Put grated ginger and minced garlic on top of the meat. Plunk this mass into a hot sizzling oiled skillet or *wok*. This takes care of pre-frying the ginger and the garlic, as most recipes tell you and yet the rest of the pan is already busy cooking the meat. This method accomplishes the cooking faster and there is less smoking in the kitchen!

Some ovens are very hot at 350°F. and others are moderate so reduce or increase to take care of this difference. Adjust your oven's heating manners!

How to tell rice sticks and bean threads apart when you have them stored and do not have the original wrappers. Rice sticks will freely crumble in your hand whereas bean threads are tough and hard to break apart. The rice stick is a bit whiter in appearance and the bean thread is a more grey, opaque shade. When cooked, the bean thread is chewy while the rice stick is like rice in texture.

Always broil fish with the skin side towards the broiler so that the fat under the skin will run between sections of the fish to make it moist and succulent. Turn over 5 minutes before serving to brown surface.

Spank pork to tenderize it.

If you want a shiny look to your sweet and sour sauce stir in a little oil just before taking off the stove and serving.

Use the Oriental grater for citrus rinds. Won't clog up holes since the grater is holeless. It has a roughened surface which does the grating and if particles get plugged you can always use the pastry brush to make full use of the gratings.

To shred green onions, remove root ends and with a sharp paring knife slash lengthwise 4 or 5 times, then, cut crosswise at 1½-inch lengths or whatever you like. A lot of thin shreds result this way.

Chicken and duck feet are stewed or fried by the Chinese and are very delicious. Especially valued by women who have just given birth for its high nutritional value. Once my husband's friend ordered "Chicken Feed"—we were surprised to see feet! We thought a "feed" was coming. We misunderstood. Actually this is no different from eating and munching on pig's feet. Sort of gelatinous texture.

Watermelon seeds are roasted by the Chinese and eaten as we do sunflower seeds.

Partially freeze your meat for easier slicing.

Do not use Japanese *dashi* (seaweed and fish soup base) for Chinese foods. You'll end up with Japanesey-Chinese flavors! Most damaging! Especially to a knowledgeable gourmet's taste buds.

An old Oriental saying goes: It is better that a man wait for his food rather than the food wait for him.

When using one of the new Japanese sno-cone ice shavers use Hawaiian punch base. It is not so sugary as the imitation syrups that are sold and you will benefit from real fruit flavors. By the way, get the sturdy upright style with metal frame. It has a good place to grasp when you are operating it. This is a marvelous gift for a child and mother can borrow it for the daiquiris when she wants to.

Leftover *chow mein* is almost like leftover spaghetti—better the next day!

If you have unexpected guests, Oriental food has tremendous advantages. You can stretch nicely—just improvise and invent another dish. Be a vivacious actress or breezy actor. Be calm, smile and serve!

Never use powdered ginger for Oriental cookery. Always fresh or frozen tubers. There is no relationship in flavor at all to canned ginger spice. Better to leave out if you do not have any.

Save your leftover rice. Keep in the refrigerator and after a few days make fried rice.

Oriental cooks have a great reverence for food and nothing

is wasted, they have been practicing "food ecology" for centuries. Use the celery tops, the cauliflower stems and leaves, the outer green lettuce leaves—whether you are rich or poor.

Fry a piece of ginger and garlic in your used, filtered oil to remove fish odors.

Garlic and ginger add flavor, but also neutralize undesirable flavors.

Odor of fish is removed by the use of vinegar or lemon juice. Sherry, ginger and garlic used while cooking help to mask fish smells.

Use a heavy plastic bag to marinate bulky pieces of meat.

If a recipe calls for 1 lb. of meat and you have 1¼ lbs. or 1⅓ lbs. go ahead and use it—do not begin to alter the seasonings. Meat and vegetable measurements are not so exacting. Keep everything in proportionate balance, however. Do this after you are more familiar. At first, follow directions to the letter!

Bean sprouts and bamboo shoots do not freeze well. The flavor is there but the crunchiness gets lost.

Japanese salted pickles are considered an aid to digestion, especially, after fried foods and rice. Pickles are even served for breakfast in Japan, along with *miso* soup. Modern Japanese breakfasts are westernized and coffee, bread, ham and eggs in the larger cities are quite common.

Dare to try some of the unusual. Read and experiment with cook books. When I began over 25 years ago there was nothing. Anything worthwhile in life is worth working for. Seek out vibrant flavors and let your taste buds just sing!

Western adaptation of Oriental foods. Have one main dish and increase the quantity of same if it is that kind of entree which can be safely increased.

Overcooking your vegetables like cauliflower, cabbage, broccoli and brussels sprouts result in strong odors. Prepared the Oriental style they are almost of sweet fragrance and definitely not like the odoriferous cabbage when cooked too long.

If your bunch of broccoli is large, use the stems peeled for one dish and save the flowers for another time.

Do not use soy indiscriminately. Too much is not good for your health, it is too salty and hard on the heart.

Expensive water chestnut flour results in a very crispy coating for deep-fat frying and is the choice of genuine Chinese cooks.

Excessive use of MSG is detrimental, but it has been proven in laboratory tests to be harmless to use in dashes and pinches! It is not a manmade chemical, but a natural derivative of agricultural products.

Aburage or fried bean cake freezes well.

Do not feel you have to always arrange everything in Japanese cooking artistically. Sometimes we have time only to make piles of our ingredients on a tray or even just on the cutting board. Feel free to do as you like. There are no rigid rules.

When cutting *makizushi* (rolled seaweed with vinegared rice) use a rather thin blade knife. Between cuts pull blade through a piece of *daikon* (Japanese radish) to clean the bits of sticky rice that might have adhered to the knife blade.

Daikon has a medicinal value and the diastase in it aids digestion.

Scandinavians have raw fish specialties and look at our raw steak tartare balls! So why not the Japanese with their raw fish (*sashimi*). The Chinese also have a special raw fish salad and it, too, is elegant tasting.

Taro can be fried or boiled like our russet potatoes.

Use the highest heat you have on your stove for Chinese cooking. The ideal is a built-in gas *wok* burner!

I keep commercial chicken broth with 2 holes punched like canned milk in the refrigerator. Whenever I need some stock, I pour what I need. The fat globules will remain solid and will not come through the holes. Less fat in the diet!

Improvise a steamer by taking an old, deep pan with a cover and punch a lot of holes in the bottom. Fit it over another pot so steam cannot escape. Or, place a round cake rack inside of your *wok* pan and cover.

A clean dish towel placed under the cover when steaming prevents droplets from going into your foodstuffs.

Use 2 clean, large squares of fine mesh cheesecloth (size of a man's handkerchief), one on top of the other as a duster. Put instantized flour in center of open cloth. Tie at top like a sachet bag. Use like a powder puff while making your meat buns, rolling cookies or bread doughs.

Fill empty TV dinner aluminum trays with leftover Oriental foods, especially the types that you know freeze well. Be sure to put a little rice on the tray, too. Tightly cover with foil. Label, if you like but as an element of unknown expectation, you could label it "surprise." After you get enough trays for your family, have a drawing or a TV dinner swap!

Miscellaneous Hints:

I find the *teriyaki* long skewers most handy. I clean out the spray head of my "rain bird" sprinkler when a small piece of gravel gets clogged in it. The long, thin stick fits where nothing else works! Keep a few stuck in the ground near your water source. It can be a makeshift stick to support a weak flower plant, too.

To invert a fabric tubing while sewing, especially a very thin one, I have used a long *teriyaki* stick, although for fatter tubing, I like to use a long chopstick.

There are many different lengths of skewers so keep several sizes on hand.

As Oriental-American children growing up in Oakland, California, we used to fool our friends by saying, "We can eat black paper. . . ." Actually, it was black *nori* seaweed.

When ordering in a Japanese restaurant, never get *tempura* and *tendon* together. You will find that you will get 2 orders— one a dish of *tempura* and a separate bowl of rice; the other, one bowl with rice, *tempura* and broth poured over.

The Japanese use psychology in serving the proper foods in the proper season with the proper atmosphere. Your appreciation of nature becomes more significant this way.

The bright flame-colored tangerine is a symbol to the Japanese of the rising sun and at New Year's especially, it is a gay thought to know that spring is not far away.

The steers for mouth-melting world-famed Kobe beef so highly prized for *sukiyaki* live under T.L.C., tender loving care. They get hand massages and are fed Japanese beer and special foods like rice and soy beans.

For the true enjoyment of an Oriental dried mushroom do not talk while you eat it, the flavor will be ruined. Chew it ever so slightly, pressing out the juices between the tongue and the teeth. The thick-capped ones are the best, especially if left whole. Sometime, when you feel particularly extravagant, make a dish just with these succulent mushrooms and flavorings, maybe with a bit of pork for meat. It is one of the "savored" epicurean delights of this world. Just indescribable.

The longer the noodle, the longer the life, so take one long breath to suck it in. Chinese eat noodles especially at birthday parties—for long life!

Red with gold signifies happiness and good luck in Chinese. Gifts are wrapped in red, so gay! They use characters like happiness written twice to mean double happiness or wonderful marriage. A marvelous philosophy!

Steamed white thousand layer buns for Peking duck served at wedding parties are imprinted in red food coloring with the character for double happiness, a delightful custom. The Chinese calligraphy for happiness is as shown:

one happiness

double happiness or happy marriage
(naturally, the 2 happinesses
together!)

Eat a persimmon to prevent a hangover, 30 minutes before you have your drinks. Now, to find a persimmon!

An electric rice cooker as well as many Oriental tools, pots, utensils, lacquer ware, tea sets and vases make marvelous wedding gifts. They most likely will not be duplicated.

If you get a fish bone stuck in your throat, quickly get a big lump of hot rice and swallow it. (Japanese rice works the best since it is gummy and apt to stay in one glob better.) It sort of catches the bone as it goes down and the trouble is relieved. Once down it is taken care of by your digestive juices. Of course, this is only for a tiny bone, nothing can help the big kind except a quick trip to the doctor. Be careful next time!

Chopsticks are the ideal tool for eating fish since you can remove the bones with such ease. In eating one whole fish, such as a sardine . . . hold the fish with the back portion up and press down with the side of the chopsticks all the way down the back top area. Make a tear in the skin at the top part. This will help to separate the flesh from the bones. Open the back halves now and grasp the entire set of bones from the tail area and lift off. It was easy wasn't it?

To add an Oriental flair put exotic sounding names to your Asian dishes such as "Imperial Red and Green," "Phoenix Chicken," "Snowflake," "Spring Flower," "Cloudy Dawn," "Peony Blossoms," "Wisteria Charm"—stoke the fires of your imagination.

Remove with care any lids on soup bowls at a traditional Japanese dinner. They are easily placed on the bowl, but, occasionally, removing them without spilling is quite a maneuvering process. Once at a dinner party, one of the guests tried in vain to remove her lid on the lacquered soup bowl. Such a suction had formed from the vacuum that there was quite a bit of discussion over the table as to how she should attack the lid. With some careful tapping and tipping, finally it was eased off. A most unpredictable predicament!

Chinese emphasize "good eating, good flavor and good humor" at their meals.

Whole fish is served in the Orient. In Chinese custom, especially, the head of the fish is given to the honored guest since the tastiest morsels are around the eyes.

How to pick a good restaurant? Go where you see Orientals going. They know!

If food is left over at a restaurant meal, ask for a doggie bag;

probably a dragon box would be a more suitable nomenclature, since they'll come out with box containers. This is not considered poor etiquette—on the contrary, it is a compliment to the chef.

For a make-shift grater, use an aluminum pie pan—puncture holes in bottom and use the rough side for a grater. It works! Also, can be used as a strainer.

To become a dedicated Oriental gourmet cook or "taster-eater," visit Oriental shops. There are all kinds, grocers, fortune cookie and noodle manufacturers, *tofu*-making shops—ask around, really discover and explore. Fun!

Oriental-style cooking will have a gigantic impact on your entire family diet and above all, on their continued good health. It's healthy eating!

If shrimps have shells left on in a dish and often Orientals serve them this way, it is quite permissible in Chinese etiquette to shell the shrimp with your tongue and teeth and spit out the shell. Quite a feat, though. Try it next time.

Much of the Chinese cooking in the United States has been of the Cantonese school but now there are quite a lot of different regional cooking styles being introduced in the larger cities like New York, San Francisco and Los Angeles. Dare to try them all—they are intriguing and fascinating. Some are bland, others are as peppery as the hottest chili pepper you have ever eaten. There is even a sour-hot soup!

Osmanthus fragrans (sweet olive) is found in many Oriental gardens. It is a lovely evergreen shrub and has the most delicate golden flower with sweet perfume. This "flavoring" is used for a special dessert by the Chinese. If you happen to have one of these in your garden, you will truly enjoy it. It gives the whole area a most elegant, rich, warm fragrance. It is a favorite of mine. A small branch with blossom placed in a bud vase will veil the entire room with a heavenly misty scent.

The Japanese have many words in their modern vocabulary which are actually foreign words. In fact, English words have been taken over in wholesale fashion! It might surprise you how much "Japanese" you already know. For example: *bata* for butter, *omoretsu* for omelet, *desato* for dessert and *biru* for beer.

Ita daki masu—the Japanese say before eating—loosely

translated, "I will receive this food with thanks." You will hear the hostess reply, *"Dozo."* Meaning, "Please partake." After finishing your meal you would reply, *"Gochi so sama deshita."* "Thanks, again, for the meal."

At the Oriental food stores you can buy *Ame,* a candy like our caramel. It is eaten paper and all—not really paper but made of edible ingredients and resembles a clear cellophane wrap. Kids think it very jolly fun to be able to eat paper. Try some.

Four is a quantity not used in things Japanese since the phonetic sound is the same as for the word for death.

There are countless traditions and superstitions in Oriental cultures. It would be impossible to learn them all for practical use in America. Most of them would not suit our way of life. Use your common sense and live American-style. Take the best from all cultures!

Rice paper is not made from rice but from paper mulberry or bamboo.

Season a new *wok* by putting it on top of your barbecue grill as the charcoal dies down and leave overnight. Or, use the *wok* as a brazier and burn the charcoal right in it. Leave overnight in a safe place. It really seasons nice and fast! Wash well with soap and water. Scrub with steel wool and dry over heat. Rub with oil. Rub off any excess. It is now ready to use. It is indestructible.

I refer to the rolled-steel *wok*—not inexpensive aluminum ones from the discount stores.

FINALE

I still have much more to tell and I plan to write another volume soon. This book has been a labor of love, much sweat and hard work, late nights and early mornings but such a wonderful feeling for me to have finally finished what I set out to do—to write a book that will spread joy! And it has been fun for me!

My Japanese given name is written in Oriental characters as "celebration child"—Keiko. I chose to use "Kay" years ago, because so many persons called me incorrectly with pronunciations such as "k-i-e-ko" or "kee-ko" and so on, when it was really "kay-ko." The surname denotes "clear water"—the "clear" character actually is a combination of "sky blue" and "water." The idea is, if a mass of water appears to be sky blue, it is an indication that it is clear and pure.

This book is a celebration of my lifelong efforts and now I can, indeed, celebrate. And, thank you, for faithfully following me to the very end—even if you did peek here first!

I cheer you with happy cooking and as the Chinese characters denote—I bid you good luck and long life!

Translated:
Shimizu Keiko

Translated:
Long life and good luck

INDEX

Abalone
  Braised in Oyster Sauce, 165
  Canned, 164-65
  Sashimi, 163-64
  Soup, Canned, 165
Aburage, 148, 207
Aemone salad sauces, 93-96
Agar-Agar, 76, 194
Age. See Aburage
Almond
  Cookies, 194-95
  Dowfu, 195
Ame, 212
Anise, Star, 98
Appetizers, 52-65
  Bean Curd Cakes, 53
  Beef, Rolled, 53
  Candy, Chinese, with *Won Ton*
    Skins, 52
  Chicken, Sesame, 53
  Crab Filling, 52
  Diem Sum, 55-65
    Curry Savories, 57
    Egg Roll, 60-61, 64-65
    Meat Buns, 57-58
    Sui Mai, 56-57
    Won Ton, 60-63
  with *Miso* Sauce, 54
  Oranges, Daybreak, 55
  Peas, Edible-Pod, 53
  Sausage Filling, 52
  Soybeans, Roasted, 53-54
  Sweet Potato Chips, 55
  See also Hors d'Oeuvres
Asparagus, Fried, 85-86

Bacon, Chinese. *See Lop Yuk*
Bamboo Shoots, 96
Bata-Yaki, 118
Bean Curd Cakes
  Fresh, 53, 172-76
  Fried. *See Aburage*
Bean (Mung) Sprouts, 43-45
  Fried, 45
  in Tossed Salad, 44-45
Bean (Mung) Threads, 89-90, 204
  with Ham, 89-90
Bean(s), Black
  Salted, 167
  Sauce, 170
Beans (Red), Sweet, 190
Beans, String, *Aemono,* 95
Beef
  with Broccoli & Oyster Sauce,
    120-21
  Deep-Fried, Crispy, 119
  in Parchment, 121
  Rolled, 53
  Snow over the Mountain, 122
  Steak
    Balls, Gold, 116
    Flank, 115
  Teppan-Yaki, 117-18
  Teriyaki, 116-17
  with Tomatoes, 118-19
Beef dishes, 115-22
Beni-Shoga, 49
Berries, Celestial, 196
Bok Choy, 96
Bows (Baus), 57-60
Braising, 22

Bread, 16
Brussels Sprouts, 86
Buta Nabe, 126-27

Candy
    Ame, 212
    Chinese, with *Won Ton* Skins,
        52
    Ginger, 193
Char Siu, 123-24
Chard, Chinese, 96
Chawan Mushi, 139
Chayote, 68
Chestnuts, Water, 97
Chicken
    Balls, 104-5
    Boneless, Fried, with Nuts, 104
    with Cashews, 106
    and Cooked Vegetables, 128-30
    Deep-Fried, Crispy, 106-7
    in Papers, 109-10
    Raw, 163
    Roast, 5-Spices, 107
    Salad, 99-100
        Tossed, Shredded, 105
    Sesame, 53
    Steamed, and *Lop Yuk,* 134
    Sweet & Pungent, 125
    Sweet & Sour, 108
    Wings
        Boneless, Stuffed, 102-3
        Drumsticks from, 100-2
    See also Cornish Hen
Chirashi-Zushi, 149
Chop Suey, 83
Chopsticks, 30, 210
    how to use, 35-36
    varieties, 28
Chow Mein, 79-82, 205
    Pork, 80-82
Chow Yuk, 82-84
    with Cabbage, etc., 83-84
Chung Choi, 66
Cilantro, 96

Clams
    Fresh, 165-66
    Hokki, 95
Cleaver, 24-25
Cooker, Rice, 27
Cooking hints, 12-13, 15, 16, 17-18,
    201 ff.
Cooking methods, unique Oriental,
    22-23
Cornish Hen, Crisp, 113-14
Cornstarch, 202
Crab Filling, 52
Curry Savories, 57
Custard
    Clam, 139
    Steamed, 139

Daikon, 96, 182-84, 207
Dashi, 152, 205
Desserts, 188-200
    Agar-Agar, 194
    Almond
        Cookies, 194-95
        Dowfu, 195
    Bean, Sweet, 190
    Berries, Celestial, 196
    Candy, Ginger, 193
    Citrus Ginger, Icy, 192-93
    Fortune Cookies, 192
    Fruit *Shiratama,* 189
    Fruits with Ginger, 193
    Ice Cream, Ginger, 193
    Orange Tea, Sweet, 190
    Persimmons
        Dried, 199-200
        Fuyu, 198-99
        Hachiya, 196-97
    Relish, Ginger, 193
    Rice, Steamed, 190-91
    Sponge Cake, Steamed, 191-92
Diem Sum. See Appetizers
Dow Fu, 172-76
Dow See, 167

Dressing
  Salad, Oriental, 92
  for Turkey, 112
  See also Sauce(s)
Duck, Peking, 110-12

Egg Dishes
  Foo Young, 141-42, 203
  Plum Blossom, 71-73
  Raw, 141
  Tea, Marbleized, 137-39
  See also Custard; Omelet
Egg Roll, 60, 64-65
  Skins, 60
      how to revive, 61
  with Spinach, 137
Eggplant(s)
  Baked, 85
  Japanese, Fried, 84
  Oriental, 84-85
  with Sake, 85
  Slices, 84-85
Entertaining Asian style, 32-34
Envelope Wrap, Oriental, 38-39
Etiquette at table, 14, 30-31, **77**,
  211-12

Fish
  Broiled, Salted, **157**
  Raw, Sashimi, **162-63**
  Steamed, **158-59**
  Teriyaki, **157**
  See also name of specific fish
Five (5) Spices, 97
Fortune Cookies, 192
Freezing of foods, 19
Fruit(s)
  with Ginger, 193
  Shiratama, 189
  storing dried, 37
Frying
  Deep-Fat, 22
  Stir-Toss, 22

Garlic, 87-88
Garnish(es), 69, 70-74
  Cutters for, 71
  Eggs, Plum Blossom, 71-73
  Lotus Lace Flowers, 74
  Onion Spray Flowers, 71
  Tomato Roses, 73-74
  Vegetable Flowers, 73
  See also name of specific dish
Ginger, 43, 88-89, 205
  Candy, 193
  with Fruits, 193
  Ice Cream, 193
  Icy Citrus, 192-93
  Pickled, 150
Gobo, 96
Goiter, 75
Gomoku-No-Moto, 149
Grater, 27, 203-4, 211
Greens, Pickled, 186

Ham, with Cellophane Shreds, 77
Helpful Hints, 201-12
Hibachi cooking, 23
Hiyamugi, 79
Hors d'Oeuvres, 47, 49-51
  Beef, Rolled, 53
  list of, 49-51
  See also Appetizers
How-to Section, 35-48

Inari-Zushi, 149
Ingredients
  how to prepare, 20-21
  how to store, 201

Jicama, 97

Kaki, 196-200
Kakimochi Rice Chips, 47
Kamaboko, 49, 69
  Kanten, 76, 194
Katsuobushi, 53

Kim Chee, 186
Kobe beef, 209
Konbu, 76, 129

Lion's Head, 130
Lop Cheong, 133
  with Bean Cake, 135
  and Rice, 135
  Soong, 134-35
  and Steamed Chicken, 134
Lop Yuk, 133
  Stir-Fried, and *Nappa,* 135-36
Lotus Lace Flowers, 74

Mahi-Mahi, 156-57
Mai Fun, 45
Maki-Zushi, 150
Meat Buns, 57-58
Melon
  Bitter, 96
  Fuzzy, 96-97
  Winter, 97
Menu planning, 16
Mirin, 98
Miso
  Paste, 98
  Sauce, Appetizers with, 54
  Yaki, 158
Mo Gwa, 96-97
"Mock Lamb," 122
MSG (monosodium glutamate), 97, 207
Mushrooms
  Dried, 86-87, 209
  how to keep fresh, 37
Mustard Paste, 97

Nam Yoy, 97
Nappa, 97
Nigiri-Zushi, 151
Nishime, 128-30
Noodles, 77-83
  Cellophane, 89
  in *Chow Mein,* 80-83

Hiyamugi, 79
  Pan-Fried, 82-83
  Ramen, 78
  Rice, 47
  Saimin, 78
  Udon, 78-79
Nori, 76
Nori-Maki, 150
Nuts, 104, 106, 109

o-, as polite prefix, 146
Oboro, 150
O-Chazuke, 181
Oil, 16, 22, 143, 203, 206
  how to strain, 37-38
  Sesame, 143, 203
Okai, 180
Olive, Sweet, 211
Omelet, Rolled, 140-41
O-Mizutaki, 151-54
Omoretsu, 140-41
Onion Spray Flowers, 71
Orange Tea, Sweet, 190
Oranges, Daybreak, 55
Oysters
  Dried, 166
  Minced Dried, and Pork with Vegetables, 166-67

Paddle, Rice, 27-28
Parboiling, 23
Parsley, Chinese, 96
Pastries, Chinese. *See Diem Sum*
Peas, Edible-Pod, 41, 53
Peking Duck, 110-12
Peppers
  Green, Broiled, 85
  Green, Stuffed, with Black **Bean** Sauce, 169-71
  Oriental, 98
Persimmons, 196-200, 209
  Dried, 199
  Fuyu, 198-99
  Hachiya, 196-98

Pickle(s), 49, 181-87, 206
  Greens, Salted, 186
  Land & Sea, Crunchy, 187
  Mash, 185
  Radish, Yellow, 183-84
  Rakkyo, 49, 182
  Salted, with *Nappa,* 184-85
  Tokyozuke, 49, 182
Pilaf, 27
Pork, 123-36, 203, 204
  Barbecued, 123-24
  Chopped, with Vegetables, 127-28
  Chow Mein, 80-82
  and Cooked Vegetables, 128-30
  Cutlets, *Tonkatsu,* 132-33
  with *Dow Fu,* 132
  Lion's Head, 130
  and Oysters with Vegetables, 166-67
  in a Pot, 126-27
  Sausage. *See Lop Cheong*
  Spareribs, Barbecued, 131-32
  Sweet & Pungent, 125-26
  with Water Chestnuts, *Ma Tai Soong,* 130-31
Pork dishes, 123-36
Potato, Japanese, 41
Poultry dishes, 99-114

Rice, 16, 178-81
  Balls, 180
  Chinese, 178-79
  Chips, *Kakimochi,* 47
  Fried, 136
  Gruel *(Okai),* 180
  Japanese, 179
  and *Lop Cheong,* 135
  Noodles, Boiled or Fried, 47
  O-Chazuki, 181
  Sticks, 204
    Fried, 45-46
  Vinegared. *See Sushi*
Rice Cooker, 27
Rice Paddle, 27-28

Sai Fun, 89, 154
Sake, 98
Salad(s)
  Celery & Crab *Sunomono,* 92
  Cellophane Shreds with Ham, 77
  Chicken, 99-100
    Tossed, Shredded, 105
  Cucumber, 92-93
  Ocean, 75-76
  Sauces. *See* Sauce(s)
  Tossed, with Bean Sprouts, 44-45
  Turnips, Chrysanthemum-Shaped, 90-91
  Watercress & Bean Sprout, 91-92
Salmon
  Miso-Yaki, 158
  Soaked in *Sake* Lees, 181
Salt, 202
Saltpeter, 124
Samoji, 27-28
Sauce(s)
  Black Bean, 170
  Hoisin, 97
  Miso, 54
  Oyster, 98, 120
  Salad
    Oriental, 92
    Sesame, Sweet & Sour, 96
    Soy, Sweet, 95
    Sumiso, Velvety, 94-95
  Soy, 12, 98, 207
  Sweet & Sour, 102
  See also name of specific dish
Sausage
  Chinese. *See Lop Cheong*
  Filling, 52
Seafood dishes, 156-71
Seaweed
  dishes with:
    Cellophane Shreds with Ham, 77
    Ocean Salad, 75-76
  how to use, 75
  Toasted, 105

varieties, 75-76
Servings in recipes, 19
Sesame Seeds
how to toast, 36
for pincushions, 36-37
Sha Ho Fun, 47
Shabu-Shabu-Nabe, 152-54
Shee Soong, 166-67
Shibui, 31
Shio-Yaki, 157
Shopping hints, 15
Shrimp
Cantonese, 167-69
Dry-Fried, 159-60
Fritters, 160-61
how to clean, 39-40
in Lobster Sauce, 167-69
Shrimp-Flavored Chips, 47
Shungiku, 97
Simmering, 22
Skimmer, Wire, 28, 144
Snow over the Mountain, 122
Soup(s), 30-31, 66-69
Base, 66-67
Cloudy Mist, 68
Egg Drop (Flower), 66
Fish, 68
Greens, 67
Noodle. *See* Noodles
Tranquil Beauty, 68-69
Winter Melon, 67-68
Soy (Sauce). *See* Sauce(s), Soy
Soybean(s), 172-74
Curd Cake, 172-76
Homemade, 175-76
Paste, 98
Roasted, 53-54
Sponge Cake, Steamed, 191-92
Squash, Fuzzy, 96-97
Squid
Deep-Fried, with Batter, 162
Fried, Crispy, 161-62
Steak. *See* Beef, Steak

Steaming, 22-23, 159, 207
Strainer, *Tempura,* 29
Sui Mai, 56-57
Sukiyaki, 154-55
Sunomono salad sauces, 90, 92, 93
Suribachi, 36
Sushi, 147-51
Aburage for, 148
Chirashi-Zushi, 149
Inari-Zushi, 149
Maki-Zushi, 150
Nigiri-Zushi, 151
Nori-Maki, 150
Sweet Potato Chips, 55

Takuwan, 183-84
Tea, 30, 176-78
Genmai, 176-77
Green, 177
Oolong, 177
Tempura, 143-46
Teppan-Yaki. See Beef, *Teppan-Yaki*
Teriyaki. See Beef, *Teriyaki;* Fish, *Teriyaki*
Tofu, 172-76
Tomato Roses, 73-74
Tools & Utensils, 24-29
Chopsticks, 28
Cleaver, 24-25
Cooker, Rice, 27
Grater, 27
Paddle, Rice, 27-28
Skimmer, Wire, 28
Strainer, *Tempura,* 29
Wok, 25-26
Spatula, 26-27
Towel, hot, 31
Turkey, Oriental-Flavored, 112
Turnips
Chrysanthemum-Shaped, 90-91
Pickled, 186-87

Utensils. *See* Tools & Utensils

Vegetable Flowers, 73
Vegetables, Oriental
  grown from seed (list), 41
  list of, 96-98

Wakame, 75-76
Wasabi, 98

Wines, 98
Wok, 25-26
  Spatula, 26-27
Won Ton, 52, 60-63
  Skins, 60-63
    how to revive, 61
"Wooly Lamb," 122